Saratoga 1777

Turning point of a revolution

Campaign • 67

Saratoga 1777

Turning point of a revolution

Brendan Morrissey • Illustrated by Adam Hook

Series editor Lee Johnson • *Consultant editor* David G Chandler

First published in Great Britain in 2000 by Osprey Publishing,
Midland House, West Way, Botley, Oxford OX2 0PH, UK
44-02 23rd St, Suite 219, Long Island City, NY 11101, USA
Email: info@ospreypublishing.com

Osprey Publishing is part of the Osprey Group.

A CIP catalog record for this book is available from the British Library

ISBN: 978 1 85532 862 4

Editor: Nikolai Bogdanovic
Consultant Editor: David G Chandler
Series Editor: Lee Johnson
Design by Black Spot
Birds-eye view battlemaps by Paul Kime
Cartography by Map Studio
Origination by Grasmere Digital Imaging, Leeds, UK
Printed in China through World Print Ltd

12 13 14 15 16   21 20 19 18 17 16 15 14 13 12

The Woodland Trust
Osprey Publishing is supporting the Woodland Trust, the UK's
leading woodland conservation charity, by funding the dedication
of trees.

www.ospreypublishing.com

Editor's note

The footnotes referred to in the text are provided at the end of
each chapter.

Artist's note

Readers may care to note that the original paintings from which the
color plates in this book were prepared are available for private sale.
All reproduction copyright whatsoever is retained by the Publishers.
All enquiries should be addressed to:

Scorpio Gallery
PO Box 475
Hailsham
East Sussex
BN27 2SL
UK

The Publishers regret that they can enter into no
correspondence upon this matter.

Dedication

To Patrick John George and Emmet Ian Thomas; and to Nora for
the gift of them.

Author's note

For the sake of brevity and simplicity, the white inhabitants of Great
Britain's North American colonies are called either 'Americans' or
'Loyalists', according to allegiance. In addition, the inhabitants of
Quebec province, whether of British or French stock, are described
as 'Canadians', while the other peoples of the region are referred to
either by their own tribal name or collectively as 'Indians' (the term
in common usage at the time).

The term 'New York' refers to the entire colony (or state), while
the conurbation on the Manhattan peninsula is always referred to as
'New York City'.

With regard to illustrations, the author has ignored the plethora of
'heroic' 19th-century artwork in favor of images which he feels most
accurately depict the people, places, and events of the campaign.

KEY TO MILITARY SYMBOLS

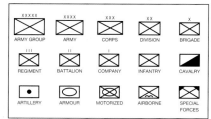

CONTENTS

COLONIAL NORTH AMERICA IN 1777

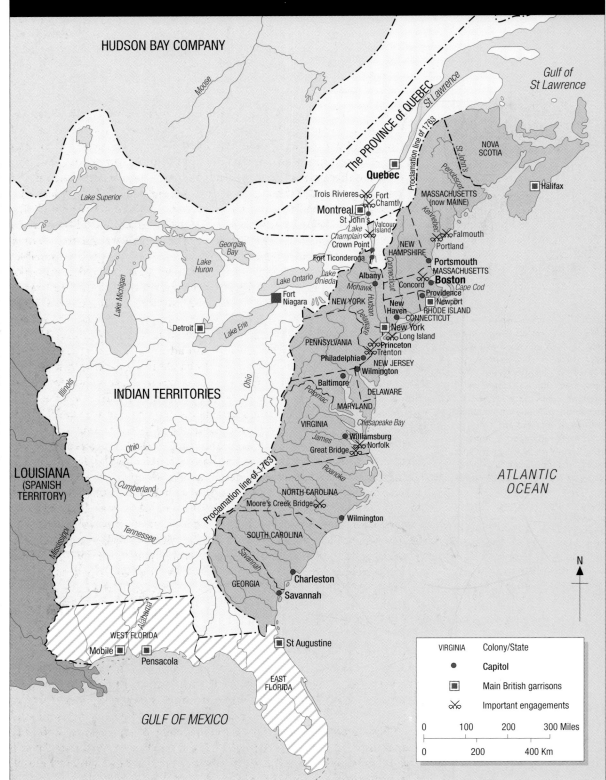

HUDSON BAY COMPANY

Moose

Gulf of St Lawrence

The PROVINCE of QUEBEC

St Lawrence

Proclamation line of 1763

NOVA SCOTIA

■ Quebec

Lake Superior

Trois Rivieres ⚔ Fort Chamtly
Montreal ■
St John's
Lake Champlain
Valcour Island
Crown Point
Fort Ticonderoga

MASSACHUSETTS (now MAINE)

Kennebec

■ Halifax

St John's

Penobscot

⚔ Falmouth
Portland

Georgian Bay

Lake Huron

Lake Michigan

Lake Ontario

Albany ●
Mohawk
Lake Oneida

NEW HAMPSHIRE

Portsmouth ■
MASSACHUSETTS
Concord Boston ■
Cape Cod
Providence ●
Newport ■
RHODE ISLAND

■ Fort Niagara

Lake Erie

NEW YORK

Hudson
Delaware

CONNECTICUT
New Haven ●

Detroit ■

New York ■
Long Island

PENNSYLVANIA

⚔ Princeton
Trenton
NEW JERSEY

INDIAN TERRITORIES

Ohio

Philadelphia ●
Wilmington ●

Baltimore ●

DELAWARE

Potomac

MARYLAND

Ohio

VIRGINIA

James
Williamsburg ●
Great Bridge ⚔
Norfolk

Chesapeake Bay

LOUISIANA (SPANISH TERRITORY)

Cumberland

Roanoke

Proclamation line of 1763

ATLANTIC OCEAN

Mississippi

Tennessee

NORTH CAROLINA
Moore's Creek Bridge ⚔

Wilmington ●

SOUTH CAROLINA

Savannah

GEORGIA

Charleston ●
Savannah ●

N ↑

Alabama

WEST FLORIDA
Mobile ■
Pensacola ■

St Augustine ■

EAST FLORIDA

GULF OF MEXICO

VIRGINIA	Colony/State
●	**Capitol**
■	Main British garrisons
⚔	Important engagements

0   100   200   300 Miles

0   200   400 Km

THE ROAD TO SARATOGA

General Sir William Howe (1729-1814). **Despite alleged blood links to the throne, Howe's Whig sympathies invariably made him a target for the government. A competent though sometimes indolent commander, he had served under Wolfe and Amherst in Canada and was an acknowledged expert in light infantry tactics. Replacing Gage as commander-in-chief, he had defeated Washington with some ease, but the events of 1777 would lead him to resign in protest at the government's lack of support for his ideas and its insistence on diverting resources to Canada to support a plan he had already advised was impracticable. (National Army Museum)**

In January 1777, the British commander-in-chief in North America, Lieutenant General Sir William Howe, wrote to the Secretary of State for the American Colonies, Lord George Germain, amending previously stated aims for the coming campaign. His previous plan[1] had involved two thrusts from Canada, each of 10,000 men, against Boston and Albany, to separate the other colonies from New England (still widely seen as the source of rebellion), while 8,000 troops held New Jersey and 7,000 garrisoned New York City and Newport. If successful, he would then attack Philadelphia in the fall, and South Carolina and Georgia that winter. However, recent losses and the realization that, even if they were available, the extra ten ships of the line and 15,000 men he wanted would never arrive in time led him to focus solely on Philadelphia, in the hope of destroying the Continental Army, capturing Congress, and thus ending the war.

Meanwhile in Pennsylvania Howe's opponent, General George Washington, was keen to discover what the British were planning. He too had reduced British options to either an advance up the Hudson River to Albany (supply base of the Northern Army) or an attack on his Main Army around Philadelphia. A co-ordinated campaign to isolate New England he considered beyond their capabilities – especially a thrust southwards from Canada. In any event, such a move would surely founder on Fort Ticonderoga, the 'Gibraltar of the wilderness'.

Unlike Washington, Major General Philip Schuyler, commanding the Northern Department, and his temporary replacement, Major General Horatio Gates, had actually visited Fort Ticonderoga: neither the fort nor its garrison were deemed fit to oppose any British attack. Despite this advice (and encouraged by a misleading report from the outgoing garrison commander), Washington refused their request for 12,000 men to defend Lake Champlain and the Mohawk Valley, arguing that reinforcing the Hudson Highlands would protect Albany against an attack from New York City. However, Schuyler and Gates had had direct experience of the enemy's ability to wage war from Canada: in contrast to Washington, they not only believed the British could do so again, but that this was precisely their plan for 1777.

The war in North America: 1775–77

The 'shot heard round the world' at Lexington on April 19 1775, had led to most of the British garrison of North America becoming trapped in Boston, and a Pyrrhic victory on Breed's Hill two months later had merely emphasized their plight. At the same time, the American Northern Army had invaded Canada, while throughout the South, rampaging Whig militias expelled Royal governors and intimidated Loyalists and neutrals alike, until isolated outposts of regulars were all that remained of the King's rule.

ABOVE, LEFT *George Sackville, Lord Germain (1716-1785), by T. Gainsborough.* **Secretary of State for the American Colonies from November 1775 to February 1782, he is usually reviled as the architect of defeat (in fact, he had organized the successful build-up of British forces in North America in 1776). However, his attempts to direct the war from London and his support for incompatible strategies did contribute to defeat at Saratoga and later Yorktown. His own dismissal from the army and his behaviour towards the Howe brothers and Carleton (all popular leaders) also meant that neither he, nor his directives received much respect from the King's forces. (The Courtauld Institute and Knowle Estates)**

ABOVE, RIGHT *General George Washington (1732-1799), by E. Leutze.* **Though often poor tactically, Washington understood the nature of the war and how to win it with the forces at his disposal, and was invariably proved correct in his choices for senior commands. However, his failure to believe that the British were capable of, let alone would attempt, an invasion from Canada (despite Carleton's near-success the previous winter) would cause the commanders of the Northern Department considerable problems. (Boston Public Library)**

The new year saw no appreciable change: despite their failure to capture Quebec, the Americans still held most of Canada and by March, had also forced the British to withdraw from Boston to Halifax. American privateers began seizing convoys of vital supplies and a badly planned attack on Charleston added to the Royal Navy's embarrassment.

However, in the second half of 1776, the tide turned. With the arrival of British and German reinforcements, the Northern Army, weakened by disease and combat, was forced to abandon Canada, and only shortages of supplies and the early onset of winter stopped the British from recapturing Crown Point and Fort Ticonderoga and controlling upper New York. Further south, August and September had seen the largest armies either side would assemble in the conflict dispute control of New York City. With superior training and naval support, the British were able to drive the Main Army from Long Island, Manhattan, and New Jersey, before winter forced them to disperse in search of food and shelter. However, this allowed the Main Army to concentrate its remaining strength (shrinking daily as enlistments expired) against isolated brigades at Trenton and Princeton. While not significant strategically, these tactical victories provided a vital and timely boost to American morale and led to the realization that they were capable of doing more than merely defending earthworks.

The view from Europe in 1777

These American successes also aroused interest in France and Spain: both were eager to avenge their losses in the Seven Years War, but they had hitherto merely been amused observers of Great Britain's colonial difficulties. Now there was an opportunity for revenge, and military supplies began to flow across the Atlantic, though neither would countenance all-out war – yet.

Elsewhere, Frederick the Great of Prussia and Catherine the Great of Russia were – though officially neutral – noticeably more hostile towards Britain. Even in those German states assisting King George (at least as long as his gold kept coming) liberals decried their rulers' 'trade' in human lives.

Britain's problems, including her isolation, increased as the war continued, and a quick, decisive blow was clearly needed. Howe had had the chance to deliver it, but mindful that too crushing a defeat might prevent conciliation subsequently, had held back. Many prominent politicians and soldiers felt that such a chance would never arise again: indeed, some had said before hostilities began, that the nature of North America and its people made any war unwinnable. Unfortunately, a much smaller – but far more influential – group, disagreed.

Footnote

1 The idea of an invasion from Canada was not new: both Howe and his predecessor as commander-in-chief, Lieutenant General Sir Thomas Gage, had proposed it in 1775, and Sir Guy Carleton, Governor of Canada, had actually attempted it in the fall of 1776.

THE SEAT OF WAR

I n 1775, New York's 50,000 square miles (including modern-day Vermont) formed a wedge between New England and the middle colonies. Mainly virgin wilderness, with few white settlements north of Fort Ticonderoga, or west of Fort Dayton, New York's socio-political development had been dictated by topography: dense forest, numerous lakes and mountain ranges cleft by two major rivers, the Hudson and the Mohawk.

The easiest way to travel was by water, and the fur trade had established two routes; either up the Hudson – navigable up to Fort Edward – to the St Lawrence, via lakes George and Champlain; or along the Mohawk to the St Lawrence, via Lake Oneida and Lake Ontario. Both routes iced over in winter (for up to six months in some places) and both involved overland journeys; ten miles from Fort Edward to Fort George for the former, and the three-mile Great Oneida Carrying Place for the latter (said to stretch to five miles when it rained). There were also numerous 'portages', where boats (and their cargo) had to be man-handled around rapids and falls. With the upper Hudson and parts of the Richelieu only navigable by shallow-draught vessels, the Mohawk route, though much longer, was by far the easier.

Land travel was difficult: even relatively short journeys were usually undertaken only in summer. Traversing the forests, even on foot, was dangerous; the leaf canopy excluded light, while centuries of leaf fall created a soggy morass, devoid of soil and littered with roots and rocks. By law, public roads had to pass through a clearing at least six rods (100 feet) wide, but even these routes were poor, and filling ruts with rushes or saplings and a covering of soil was the only form of maintenance. Lesser roads barely allowed two carriages to pass and could easily be blocked by windfalls because trees were only cut back to the width of the track. Even so-called military roads – log causeways, also called 'corduroys' – did not last long.

The weather was equally inhospitable. The hot, thundery summers were extremely unhealthy, and in winter, lakes and rivers began to freeze in November, as did the ground, sometimes down to ten feet. The late thaw (typically in early April) left roads and fields flooded with water and swarming with insects.

New York in the Revolution

New York was the seventh most populous rebel colony, with 150,000 whites (including 10,000 in Vermont), almost 20,000 free or enslaved blacks, and 10,000 Iroquois ('Six Nations') around the Great Lakes. New York City was the second largest conurbation after Philadelphia, with 22,000 inhabitants (including 3,000 slaves). Almost a quarter of the whites were not of British or Irish descent: they included Palatine and Rhineland Germans, Dutch, French Huguenots, and Swedes.

Despite its conservative image, New York led the anti-tax lobby, hosted the Stamp Act Congress, and witnessed the first bloodshed of the Revolution (the Battle of Golden Hill) and the first clear-cut success (the capture of Fort Ticonderoga and Crown Point). After Lexington, militia seized the New York City arsenal and took over the night watch, and by July, New York had raised 3,000 Continentals. Yet by 1783, the region had produced more active Loyalists than any other colony (5,000 of the estimated 25,000 who bore arms[1]). With land ownership based on the English 'manorial' system, benign landlords (as most were) could form units that were practically feudal levies. New York Loyalists produced nine complete regiments (and several smaller corps) and much of the manpower for two others: in contrast, the Continental Line comprised two short-lived 'additional' corps, four infantry regiments, and two artillery companies.

The region's history guaranteed that upper New York contained many veterans and its geography made it inevitable that this area would once again become a battleground. (In fact, a third of all the engagements in the war would take place in New York, and fighting continued there for a full year after Yorktown.) However, 15 years of peace had seen its military infrastructure collapse, and the hard-won knowledge of how to fight and – equally importantly – live in this wilderness had largely been lost to the British (though not, as it would later transpire, to their foes).

Footnote

1 Contrary to popular myth, few Loyalists were Royal 'placemen' or rich merchants: at least half appear to have been farmers – many of them veterans of colonial wars given land grants as a pension – while others were artisans (a social group usually presented as entirely anti-British), political dissidents, religious and ethnic minorities (especially Scots and Irish Catholics), or those for whom rebellion represented a step too far towards treason.

THE OPPOSING COMMANDERS

Major General John Burgoyne (1722-92) by Sir J. Reynolds. **In London, Burgoyne boasted that he would return victorious within a year. (The Frick Collection)**

Lieutenant General Sir Henry Clinton (1738-95), by J. Smart. **Always a difficult subordinate, Clinton was upset when Burgoyne, his junior, was given command of the Canadian army, though he refused a post as the latter's nominal superior. (National Army Museum)**

THE BRITISH AND GERMANS

Lieutenant General John Burgoyne (1722-92) was commissioned into the cavalry at 15 and served in the War of the Austrian Succession, but left the army in 1751, after eloping with the Earl of Derby's daughter. Subsequently reconciled with his father-in-law, whose patronage helped re-establish his career, Burgoyne saw his first action at St Malo and then served at Cherbourg, Belle-Ile, and the famous raid on Valencia de Alcantara. He later became Member of Parliament for Preston and governor of Fort William. Promoted to major general in 1772, he arrived in Boston in May 1775, but returned home that winter when his wife fell ill. In 1776, he took a strong Anglo-German reinforcement to Canada and pestered Carleton to let him attack Albany, via the Great Lakes and Mohawk Valley, but when his wife's death took him back to England for another winter, he used the time to ingratiate himself with Carleton's enemy, Germain.

On February 28, 1777, at the request of the King and Germain, Burgoyne submitted his grandiosely titled 'Thoughts for Conducting the War on the Side of Canada', in which he proposed to split the colonies by a thrust down Lake Champlain to seize Albany, where he would be joined by a second force which would arrive from the Mohawk Valley, and a third coming up from New York City. The combined force would invade New England and destroy the seat of rebellion. The final phase was discarded, but the two thrusts from Canada were approved (possibly on the advice of General Amherst, a veteran of operations in North America) and Burgoyne was chosen to lead them.

While Burgoyne's treatment of the ordinary soldier was ahead of its time and earned him the sobriquet 'Gentleman Johnny', his military and literary careers were remarkably similar, both deriving from one spectacular success amidst a sea of averageness, characterized by flowery words and gestures, but often little substance. Though in every sense a gallant officer, he was also 'vain, boastful, and superficial, and not a man to depend on in a tight corner' – as subsequent attempts to excuse his defeat showed – and he clearly misunderstood the character and the politics of both the American people and the rebellion.

Major General William Phillips (1731-81) joined the Royal Artillery in 1746 and by 1758 was a captain in Germany, where meritorious service at Minden and Warburg led to his promotion over more senior colleagues. He arrived in Canada with Burgoyne in 1776, with the local rank of major general, and became Burgoyne's second-in-command and a trusted advisor. He was the senior British officer in the Convention Army, acquiring a reputation for 'blustering arrogance' (mainly for

Major General Friedrich Baron von Riedesel (1738-1800). **Just 38 in 1777, Riedesel was an energetic leader. A dutiful subordinate, he also knew when to defer to more experienced inferiors. (Fort Ticonderoga Museum)**

Colonel Barry St Leger (1737-89), by Sir J. Reynolds. **St Leger refused to believe that Fort Stanwix had been repaired. (The Courtauld Institute and The National Trust)**

condemning American ill-treatment of his men) and although paroled in November 1779, he was not officially exchanged until October 1780. Much liked by Clinton, he subsequently led raids on Rhode Island and later (with Benedict Arnold) into Virginia, where he died of typhoid fever.

Major General Baron Friedrich von Riedesel (1738-1800) was a Hessian law student who ran away to join the army. In the Seven Years War he served in England, then became ADC to the Duke of Brunswick, later transferring into his service. Chosen to lead the first division of Brunswickers sent to America, he arrived in Quebec in June 1776 and was joined a year later by his wife and children (who followed him through the campaign). Despite Burgoyne's aloofness towards him, Riedesel gave sound advice and distinguished himself in action. He spent three years in captivity, only being exchanged (together with Phillips) in October 1780. With the local rank of lieutenant general, he briefly commanded the Long Island garrison, then returned to Canada, where he remained until ordered back to Brunswick in August 1783. From 1787 to 1793, he led a Brunswick contingent in the Netherlands, and he was commandant of the city of Brunswick until his death.

Brigadier General Barry St Leger (1737-89), a Cambridge graduate, entered the army in 1756 and saw action at Louisburg, Quebec, and Montreal, acquiring a reputation for leadership in frontier warfare. By 1776, he was lieutenant colonel of the 34th Foot and, with the local rank of brigadier general, led a force down the Mohawk Valley to rally Loyalists and join Burgoyne at Albany. After 1777, he commanded ranger companies based at Montreal (one of which tried to capture Schuyler), and he remained in Canada as commander of British forces until 1785, when he left the army.

THE AMERICANS

Major General Philip Schuyler (1733-1804) was a wealthy landowner from a distinguished Dutch 'patroon' family. A regular captain in the French and Indian Wars, he fought at Lake George and subsequently at Fort Ticonderoga and Frontenac, but it was as deputy quartermaster general to the British forces in New York that he learned lessons vital to conducting military operations in the northern wilderness.

Inheriting substantial estates after the war, he was elected to the New York Assembly. In 1775, political considerations led to his appointment as major general and commander of the Northern Department. Chosen to lead the invasion of Canada, his insistence on discipline made him enemies among the 'liberal' New Englanders. An attack of gout left Montgomery de facto commander and Schuyler organizing supplies and building the Lake Champlain fleet that later forestalled Carleton.

ABOVE, LEFT *Major General Philip Schuyler (1733-1804), by J. Trumbull.* **A piercing eye and commanding air reinforced Schuyler's stern, patrician nature. (New York Historical Society)**

ABOVE, RIGHT *Major General Arthur St Clair (1737-1818), by C.W. Peale.* **Born into the Scots gentry, St Clair's military career was undistinguished: the abandonment of Fort Ticonderoga was probably his finest achievement. (Independence National Historical Park)**

Major General Horatio Gates (1727-1806), by C.W. Peale. **Usually ridiculed as a poor commander and a petty, inverted snob, Gates shared Schuyler's organizational talents but also possessed a common touch that gave him an advantage in dealing with New Englanders. (Independence National Historical Park)**

Factional politics saw his replacement by Gates in March 1777 (which, typically, he saw as an attack on his integrity): he was reinstated, but replaced again by Gates that August and had to wait a year before a court martial acquitted him of incompetence. He resigned in April 1779, to return to politics and chaired committees reorganizing military administration and co-operating with the French. After the war, he participated in public life until 1798.

Major General Arthur St Clair (1737-1818), a native Scot, joined the 60th Foot in 1757, serving at Louisburg and Quebec. In 1762, he resigned and moved to Boston, but later purchased 4,000 acres in western Pennsylvania, thereby acquiring considerable influence and becoming a colonel in the militia. As colonel of the newly-formed 2nd Pennsylvania Regiment, he joined the Northern Army and fought at Trois Rivières. Promoted to brigadier general in August, he moved south and fought at Trenton and Princeton. Further promotion in February 1777 returned him to the Northern Department as commander of Fort Ticonderoga. Given an inadequate garrison and lackluster subordinates, he abandoned the fort, but was cleared of negligence by a court martial in 1778. He later served under Sullivan against the Iroquois and, on the disbandment of the army in 1783, entered Congress. Appointed governor of the North-West Territory and commander-in-chief of the new US Army, he was defeated by the Miami in 1791 and resigned after being refused a court of inquiry. Although a later congressional investigation cleared him and he published a defense of his Indian campaign, he died in poverty.

Major General Horatio Gates (1727-1806), the godson of Horace Walpole, joined the 20th Foot in 1744, serving with Sackville (Germain) and Wolfe, and later, in a regiment raised for the Jacobite Rebellion, with John Burgoyne (coincidentally, both were also believed to be illegitimate sons of noblemen). Gates then served in Canada, before purchasing an independent company in New York in 1754. Wounded at Monongahela, he defended Fort Herkimer and served at Martinique, before retiring as a half-pay major. Settling in Virginia, he met Washington, who made him his adjutant general in 1775. He transferred to the Northern Department, serving Schuyler well before rejoining Washington for the New Jersey campaign. Early in 1777, he again went north, this time to replace Schuyler, but this appointment was later rescinded, at which he almost destroyed his career with a ranting polemic to Congress.

The fall of Fort Ticonderoga and Schuyler's retreat saw him restored once more to favor, and to the command of the Northern Army. Despite his rows with Arnold and questions in Congress over the generosity of the Convention, his victory coincided with Washington's defeats in Pennsylvania and led to moves to make him commander-in-chief. Washington subsequently opposed Gates' appointment to command the Southern Department, which ended in the disaster at Camden. Gates retired to his farm until an inquiry in 1782 cleared him of misconduct.

ABOVE, LEFT *Major General Benedict Arnold (1741-1801), by A. Cassidy.* **Arnold was never happier than when in the thick of the action, but was a troublesome subordinate away from it. (Frick Art Reference Library)**

ABOVE, RIGHT *Brigadier General John Stark (1728-1822), after S. Morse.* **Stark's battlefield bravery and leadership redeemed a fierce independence that upset his superiors as much as it did the enemy. (Independence National Historical Park)**

Major General Benjamin Lincoln (1733-1810), by C.W. Peale. **The victory at Bennington owed much to Lincoln's careful handling of the insubordinate Stark. (Independence National Historical Park)**

Then he rejoined the army. He remarried in 1786 and, after freeing his slaves, moved to New York, where he served a term in the legislature and used his wife's money to aid veterans.

Major General Benedict Arnold (1741-1801) ran off to fight in the French and Indian Wars at 15, but later deserted, re-enlisted, and then deserted again in order to complete an apprenticeship. By 1775, he was a prosperous merchant and captain of Connecticut militia. He marched to Cambridge at the outbreak of war, talking his way into commanding the attack on Fort Ticonderoga (though Allen refused to accept Arnold's authority). After capturing St John's, Washington chose him to lead one of the columns invading Canada, but the campaign was a personal disaster, ending in him being badly wounded and later losing the Lake Champlain fleet at Valcour Island.

Embittered at subordinates being promoted over his head, Arnold resigned in July 1777. Although Washington persuaded him to accept a posting to the Northern Army Department, and he relieved Fort Stanwix, his clash with Gates at Saratoga saw him relieved of command. A year-long convalescence saw a posting to Philadelphia, marriage to the daughter of a prominent Loyalist, and his first contact with British agents. Under British colors, he led a raid into Virginia (handing over command to Phillips), but was just as widely distrusted. After the war, he turned to privateering, then commerce, but he died deep in debt, leaving his wife to raise their four sons (all of whom joined the British army) and also care for the three children from his first marriage and his maiden sister.

Brigadier General John Stark (1728-1822) was a native of New Hampshire. Kidnapped for ransom by Indians as a child, he later became a captain in Rogers Rangers during the French and Indian Wars, before raising the 1st New Hampshire regiment and commanding the vital left flank at Bunker Hill. The following year, he served at Trenton and Princeton, but was ignored for promotion and resigned. Reprimanded by Congress for refusing to serve under Lincoln and Gates, he was appointed a Continental brigadier-general for defeating Baum and blocking Burgoyne's escape. Subsequent service included twice commanding the Northern Department; a planned invasion of Canada in 1778; operations in New Jersey; and the trial of Major André. Breveted major general in September 1783, he retired from public life after the war and a large farm and 11 children kept him occupied until his death.

THE OPPOSING FORCES

THE BRITISH AND THEIR ALLIES

Of the three 'British' forces in the northern campaigns of 1777, only Sir Henry Clinton's possessed a majority of British regulars (compared to 45 per cent of Burgoyne's and barely 15 per cent of St Leger's). It was the first campaign in which Loyalists were used as front line soldiers rather than as camp guards or guides while Burgoyne and St Leger also employed Canadians and Indians (the latter providing the Americans with an ideal propaganda opportunity). Given the British Army's record of handling allies, this alone boded ill for the coming campaign: other limitations – mainly organizational and logistical – stacked the odds even higher.

(1) Burgoyne's 'Canada Army'

Burgoyne's command has been called everything from 'an élite and well equipped force' through 'a mixed bag' to an army that 'made less effort to prepare itself for American campaigning than had Braddock's'. Of his 9,500 men, 4,000 were British infantry (whose organization is covered in Campaign 37 *Boston 1775*). Six of his seven regiments – and the three others that provided flank companies – had arrived in Canada the previous summer: only the 47th Foot had seen action since 1762. Indeed, with units dispersed to find food and shelter, only Fraser's Advance Corps had even trained above regimental level, although two of the light companies (the 21st and 29th) had been taught new tactics by Howe in 1774, and three more (the 9th, 20th, and 34th) had learned them later, in Ireland.

Aware that he might have to undertake at least one siege, Burgoyne acquired a large artillery train – a sensible move, given that his enemy's main tactic to date had involved fighting from behind prepared defenses. The gunners included 250 men from the Royal Artillery and Royal Irish Artillery, but while the allocation of men per gun did meet 'paper' requirements for once, there were problems finding enough draught horses, with only 237 of the 400 needed ever becoming available. Worse still was the shortage of supply wagons: of the 500 and 1,000 horses ordered, barely 200 and 400, respectively, were obtained. Many of the wagons were built hurriedly, from unseasoned wood, and they proved highly susceptible to damage from weather and the rough roads. Also, they were a two-wheeled Canadian design, which could carry less weight than the four-wheeled European type.

Burgoyne's 'German' contingents came from Brunswick (Braunschweig-Wolfenbüttel) and Hesse-Hanau. In January 1776, in the first treaty between Great Britain and various German princes, Brunswick agreed to provide 4,300 men. The corps – a dragoon regiment, four

Privates, Regiments Specht and Riedesel, by F von Germann.
Contrary to popular myth the Germans were not only generally good troops, but were also reasonably well clothed. (Miriam and Ira D Wallach Division, New York Public Library)

Private, Regiment Erbprinz (Hesse-Hanau), by F. von Germann.
The Hesse-Hanau contingent was one of only two serving alongside the British in which the tax liabilities of the soldiers' families were reduced (the other was Hesse-Kassel). This regiment spent the whole campaign guarding the artillery park and baggage. (Miriam and Ira D Wallach Division, New York Public Library)

infantry regiments, a grenadier battalion, and a light battalion (including a jaeger company) – was trained, organized, and armed along Prussian lines. The dragoons – four troops each of four officers, seven NCOs, two musicians, and 60 men, plus staff – served as a headquarters guard: one troop was eventually mounted. The four infantry (musketeer) regiments had five 'line' companies and a grenadier company that was detached to the 'converged' grenadier battalion. Apparently, some had light companies, but these did not form the light battalion, which was a separate corps formed in Brunswick.

Another treaty, with Duke Wilhelm of Hesse-Hanau (son of the ruler of Hesse-Kassel), produced a 900-strong contingent comprising an artillery company (128 all ranks), an infantry regiment (668 all ranks), and a jaeger detachment. The jaegers were later expanded to 400, though how many of the balance were raw recruits is debatable. The gunners used British guns, including four 6pdrs which had been captured at Quebec in 1759.

The Loyalists comprised two regimental cadres, under Ebenezer Jessup of New York and John Peters of Connecticut. Both expected to recruit heavily as they moved south, but most Loyalists had already fled to Canada or New York City, and those remaining in situ were unwilling to 'come out' in case royal authority proved transient. However both units fought well and, with many locals in their ranks, proved reliable guides; but constant attrition from leading the Advance Corps created gaps that proved impossible to fill (especially when Burgoyne drafted their best recruits into his depleted British units).

Burgoyne also demanded '1,000 or more savages' (whom he considered vital to his plan), but got fewer than 500, commanded by two former French officers, Charles de Langlade and the Chevalier La Corne St Luc. Drawn from a dozen nations – including Ottawas, Chippewas, Sioux, Sac, Fox, and Winnebagoes, as well as Iroquois and Algonquins – they were expected to be the eyes of the army. Those from the Detroit and Michilimackinac departments were strangers to the region, and also less 'softened' by contact with white people. Required to forego their more gruesome traditions and failing to find much booty, they deserted in such numbers that Gates' Oneidas eventually outnumbered them.

Burgoyne also requested 2,000 Canadian 'hatchet men', but recruitment was so slow that Carleton had to reintroduce the hated *corvée* (a form of forced labour): even so, desertion was endemic, and barely 300 left Canada. Attached to the Advance Corps as a type of pioneer, they were not the sharp-shooting woodsmen of Burgoyne's imagination: early setbacks left them still more demoralized and unreliable.

Finally, the Royal Navy supplied a small detachment to command the flotilla and its 700-man crew (the bateaux were rowed by Canadians, or soldiers) and to advise on bridge-building and other engineering matters.

(2) St Leger's command

St Leger's British troops comprised a few gunners, the 'picked men' of the battalion companies of the 8th Foot (which garrisoned the Great Lakes forts), and his own corps, the 34th, fresh from England. In addition, there were 80 Hesse-Hanau jaegers.

However, the vast bulk of St Leger's force was made up of native North Americans – Loyalists, Canadians, and 'Indians'. These included Sir John Johnson's 'King's Royal Regiment of New York' and a number of rangers – officers attached to the Indian Department to provide liaison, interpretation, and training in European warfare. A contingent of Canadian 'hatchet men' provided bateaux crews and working parties but added little to the fighting strength, although one militia company was present. Finally, there was an unspecified number of Iroquois – possibly as many as 1,000 – who, unlike Burgoyne's contingent, were operating on 'home ground'. However, they still displayed a lack of discipline, a tactical naivety, and a love of plunder that made them difficult if not impossible to control.

(3) Clinton's relief column

Clinton's regulars were veterans of the New York City and New Jersey campaigns, except the 7th and 26th, which had been captured in the American invasion of Canada and subsequently exchanged. His German units were also organized along Prussian lines and performed creditably: the Hessian musketeer regiment von Trumbach had also fought in the 1776 campaign. Finally, there were five Loyalist units, all newly raised but destined, together with their commanders, to earn first-class reputations in this and later campaigns.

THE AMERICANS

(1) The Continental Line

The ingrained fear of standing armies – and the practical problem of persuading men to sign on for long periods – forced Congress to rely initially on one-year enlistments. The disasters – and successes – of 1776 had showed what trained, disciplined professionals could achieve, yet despite relaxed discipline and bigger bounties, it still proved hard to persuade men to fight 'for the duration', and 1777 enlistments were kept to three years.

For 1777, Congress approved an army of 88 infantry, three artillery, and four cavalry regiments, plus 22 'additional' infantry regiments that remained 'unassigned' for political reasons. (Three such regiments served in the north: Warner's 'Green Mountain Boys' from Vermont; the 1st Canadian Regiment, composed of non-Americans; and Dubois' (5th New York), which held the Highland forts.)

Two organizational changes saw brigades become the main tactical unit ('regiments' often being of no more than company strength) and the creation of a 'light infantry' corps, raised on British lines but used in the German style to provide bayonet-armed support to riflemen. In the Northern Army, Dearborn's light infantry joined Morgan's rifle-armed 11th Virginia, creating a well balanced advance guard. Line infantry retained the 1776 (more accurately the 'November 1775') battalion organization of eight companies of four officers, four sergeants, four

Captain Pierre St Luc de la Corne. **Prominent in Canadian Indian affairs since the 1720s, and probably over 70 when the war began, St Luc was widely believed to have been involved in the Fort William Henry massacre of 1757. (National Archives of Canada - C28244)**

Joseph Brant (1742-1807), by C.W. Peale. **Born Thayendanegea, Brant grew up in the home of William Johnson and fought at Lake George – aged 13 – and later against Pontiac. Educated and deeply religious, he was far from the barbaric savage many American histories suggest. (Independence National Historical Park)**

An American Officier

An American Soldier.

ABOVE, LEFT *An American Officer*
ABOVE, RIGHT *An American Soldier,*
both by F. von Germann.

Continental infantry units were invariably short of rank-and-file, but the resulting low officer-to-man ratio may, paradoxically, have improved command and control on the battlefield. Poor's and Learned's brigades, which bore the brunt of the fighting at Saratoga, had one officer to every ten men. Despite the myths surrounding American rifles and marksmanship, most infantrymen carried smooth-bore muskets, either home-made, captured or purchased abroad. Calibers ranged from 0.65 inches (lighter Dutch muskets) to 0.80 (German types), making logistics a nightmare. Morgan's riflemen had to make their own bullets, as their weapons varied in caliber from 0.55 to 0.60 inches. (Miriam and Ira D Wallach Division, New York Public Library)

corporals, two musicians, and 76 privates, with 13 regimental staff, including three 'field' officers.

By September, the Northern Army had an independent artillery battalion of 400 men with 22 guns (having had to use 200 infantry to man the guns of Fort Ticonderoga) and there were 150 artificers. In addition, there were 250 cavalry: the terrain negated any shock value, so they mainly carried messages and guarded convoys.

(2) The militia

By 1777, it was clear that there would never be enough Continentals and that any American force would need 'bulking out' with militia, which was 'called out' for periods of between 30 and 60 days (the period specified included travel and was observed to the day, regardless of circumstances). Usually a liability – eating the army out of existence if the enemy did not turn up and creating panic if they did – they invariably fought well when defending their own homes. Mostly brigaded separately, militia units were occasionally added to Continental brigades to cover losses, as happened with every Northern Army brigade.

Bennington was won by men from New Hampshire and Vermont, but most of Gates' militia came from New York and Connecticut, although substantial New Hampshire and Massachusetts contingents arrived in mid-October. The New York militia comprised all non-exempted males between 16 and 50, with men up to 60 impressed in times of danger, as at Oriskany. They were organized in regiments of five to ten companies, formed into seven 'county' brigades, while New York City and Albany also boasted independent companies and mounted troops, usually attached to a local 'foot' regiment.

Each man brought his own musket and either a bayonet, a tomahawk, or a sword, with three pounds of powder and one of bullets. His section (one of four per company) met weekly for fours hours' drill: companies met once a month and regiments twice a year. After the Militia Act (July 1775), company officers were appointed by the rank-and-file, regimental officers by the colony. The system also provided 'levies' – ad hoc units of volunteers for short periods of emergency service. After July 1777, they were paid as Continentals while serving, but volunteers were still scarce and 'drafting' was common. Ten Broeck's brigade and the units with Gates appear to have been levies, while the Highland forts garrisons and Herkimer's force probably employed existing units.

ORDERS OF BATTLE

ANGLO-ALLIED FORCES

JUNE 1777
THE CANADA ARMY
Lt Gen John Burgoyne[1]

HEADQUARTERS

Gen Staff and Aides-de-Camp[2]	17 officers
Prinz Ludwig Dragoons – Lt Col Friederich von Baum[3]	20 / 287[4]
King's Loyal Americans – Lt Col Ebenezer Jessup	150 all ranks
Queen's Loyal Rangers – Lt Col John Peters	150 all ranks
Canadians – Capt Monin, Capt Boucherville	300 all ranks
Indians – St Luc de Lacorne and Charles de Langlade	500 in total

ARTILLERY

Royal Artillery – Maj Griffith Williams, RA (vice Phillips)   22 / 245[5]
(6th, 8th Companies, 1st Battalion and 7th Company,
3rd Battalion Royal Artillery; detachments already in
Canada from Royal Artillery and Royal Irish Artillery)

Hesse-Hanau Artillery – Capt Georg Pausch	3 / 100

Artillery Park – Capt John Carter, RA
    Right Brigade – Capt Walter Mitchelson, RA
        (Two medium 12pdrs, two 6pdrs, one 8-inch howitzer,
        one 5.5-inch howitzer)
    Center Brigade – Capt Thomas Blomfield, RA
        (Two light 24pdrs)
    Left Brigade – Capt Thomas Hosner, RA
        (Two medium 12pdrs, two 6pdrs, one 8-inch
        howitzer, one 5.5-inch howitzer)

Attached infantry – Lt George Nutt (33rd Foot)	1 / 154

RIGHT WING
Maj Gen William Phillips, RA

Royal Artillery – Capt Thomas Jones, RA
(One brigade of four 6pdrs)

Advance Corps: Brig Gen Simon Fraser (24th Foot)
Royal Artillery – Capt Ellis Walker, RA
    (Four light 6pdrs, four light 3pdrs, two 5.5-inch howitzers –
    40 infantry attached)

Corps of Marksmen – Capt Alexander Fraser (34th Foot)	4 / 98[6]
24th Foot – Maj Robert Grant[7] (vice Simon Fraser)	23 / 368

Grenadier Battalion – Maj John Acland, MP (20th Foot)   31 / 600
    (companies from 9th, 20th, 21st, 24th, 29th, 31st,
    34th, 47th, 53rd and 62nd Foot)
Light Battalion – Maj Alexander Lindsay[8] (53rd Foot)   31 / 580
    (companies from 9th, 20th, 21st, 24th, 29th, 31st,
    34th, 47th, 53rd and 62nd Foot)

1st Brigade: Brig Gen Henry Watson Powell (53rd Foot) [9]
9th Foot – Lt Col John Hill   24 / 374
47th Foot – Lt Col Nicholas Sutherland   24 / 356[10]
53rd Foot – Maj Paul Irving (vice Powell and Lindsay)   22 / 369

2nd Brigade: Brig Gen James Hamilton (21st Foot)
20th Foot (Lt Col John Lind)   23 / 360
21st Foot (Maj George Forster vice Hamilton)   23 / 370
62nd Foot (Lt Col John Anstruther)   24 / 353

LEFT WING
Maj Gen Frederick von Riedesel

Artillery [Hesse-Hanau] – Capt Georg Pausch
    (One brigade of four 6pdrs)

Advance Corps: Lt Col Heinrich von Breymann
Artillery [Hesse-Hanau] – Lt von Spangenburg
    (Two light 6pdrs and two light 3pdrs)
Grenadier Battalion – Maj Otto von Mengen (vice von Breymann)   17 / 439
    (companies from the regiments Rhetz, Riedesel, Specht
    and Prinz Friedrich)
Light Battalion – Maj Ferdinand von Barner   18 / 380
Jaeger Company – Capt Carl von Geyso (Geisau)   4 / 120

1st Brigade: Brig Gen Johann von Specht
Regiment von Rhetz – Maj Balthasar von Lucke   23 / 512
Regiment von Riedesel – Lt Col Ernst von Speth   25 / 512
Regiment von Specht – Maj Carl von Ehrenkrook[11]   24 / 512

2nd Brigade: Brig Gen Wilhelm von Gall
Regiment Prinz Friedrich – Lt Col Christian Praetorius   24 / 509
Regiment Erbprinz [Hesse-Hanau] – Lt Col von Lentz   24 / 522

Totals
Headquarters and Artillery[12]   1,900[13]
British (Advance Corps, 1st and 2nd Brigades)   4,000
Germans (Advance Guard, 1st and 2nd Brigades)   3,600
Total: 9,500

Footnotes

1 Burgoyne's and Phillips' ranks were 'local' until their promotions within the Army were confirmed on August 29: strictly speaking, it was illegal for Royal Artillery officers to command units of other arms.

2 STAFF: Adjutant and Quartermaster Gen – Lt Col Thomas Carleton (20th Foot); Deputy Adjutant Gen – Capt Robert Kingston, Irish Invalids; Deputy Quartermaster Gen (British) – Capt John Money (9th Foot); Assistant Quartermaster Gen – Capt George Vallancay (62nd Foot); Deputy Quartermaster Gen (German) – Capt Heinrich Gerlach (Regt von Specht); Judge Advocate Gen – Capt James Craig (47th Foot); Royal Engineers – Lt William Twiss; Paymaster Gen – David Geddes; Commissary Gen – Jonathan Clarke; Waggonmaster Gen – Robert Hoaksley (from July 12); Commissary and Loyalist Liaison – Col Philip Skene; Royal Navy Liaison – Lt John Schank; Artificers – Capt Wilcox, RE and Midshipman Edmund Pellew, RN. AdCs: Lt and Capt Sir Francis Clerke, Bt (3rd Guards), Capt Henry Gardiner (16th Light Dragoons), Capt Lord Petersham, MP (29th Foot); Lt Richard Wilford (2nd Dragoon Guards).

3 After Baum's death on August 16, Capt Adolph von Schlagenteuffel.

4 Wherever possible, unit strengths are shown divided between **officers** / '**other ranks**' (i.e. NCOs, privates, and musicians) to give an idea of fighting strength and command ratio. British unit strengths are from the official returns of July 1 1777, less detachments left in Canada (including sick), the grenadiers and light infantry sent to the converged battalions, and two men from every center company (but those of the 24th Foot sent to Capt Fraser's 'Rangers'. German strengths are from the returns of June 1 1777, less detachments left in Canada (including sick), and the grenadier companies, and excluding servants.

5 British/German artillery – manpower is listed under Headquarters (being detached as needed), but numbers and types of guns are listed under the formations to which they were formally assigned.

6 The strength usually quoted – 2 officers, 48 other ranks – is too low, possibly based on the assumption that the whole unit was at Bennington; in fact, it had at least three officers when it left Canada.

7 After Grant's death on July 7, Maj William Agnew.

8 Often referred to as Balcarres (of which he was the 6th Earl).

9 After the capture of Fort Ticonderoga, Burgoyne left Hamilton in command of the fort and surrounding defenses, with the 62nd Foot, Regiment Prinz Friedrich, and some gunners (in all, about 1,000 men). On August 10, the 62nd was replaced by the 53rd, and on August 15, Powell became garrison commander, with Hamilton leading the remains of the two British brigades, now merged into one formation.

10 From late August, six companies of the 47th were assigned to guard the bateaux (including supplies, landing points, and pontoon bridges) and artillery park, while two companies garrisoned Diamond Island, Lake George. This has been cited as confirmation of both its poor reputation and its reliability!

11 Not to be confused with Lt Col Johann von Ehrenkrook (Regiment von Rhetz), who remained at Trois Rivières, in command of the battalion of detachments left behind in Canada.

12 Burgoyne's artillery train, showing different calibers, numbers of each, and where assigned – note, each field gun/howitzer had one ammunition wagon, carrying 100 rounds for a light 6pdr, 300 for a 3pdr, or 90 for a 5.5-inch howitzer:

Caliber	Park	Adv Gd	Right	Left	Fleet [b]	Ft George	Total
24pdrs (heavy)	16						16
24pdrs (light) [a]	2						2
12pdrs (heavy)	10						10
12pdrs (medium)	4					4	4
12pdrs (light)					1		1
6pdrs (light)	10	4	4	6		2	26
3pdrs (light) – 'pack' guns	11	4		2			17
8-inch howitzers	4					2	6
5.5-inch howitzers	2	2				2	6
13-inch mortars	2						2
10-inch mortars	2						2
8-inch mortars	2						2
5.5-inch mortars ('Royals')	4					2	12
4.4-inch mortars ('Coehorns')	8					4	12
Total							
14 different types of ordnance	**85**	**10**	**4**	**8**	**21**	**10**	**138**

a captured from the Americans in 1776 and lighter than the medium 12pdrs

b pieces left on board the fleet in addition to those carried as armament by each vessel (see below)

13 The fleet which transported Burgoyne's army south comprised:
- Ships – *Royal George* (24 iron 12pdrs) and *Inflexible* (20 iron 9pdrs)
- Brig – *Washington* (16 iron 6pdrs)
- Schooners – *Lady Maria* (14 iron 6pdrs) and *Carleton* (12 iron 4pdrs)
- Cutter – *Lee* (10 iron 4pdrs)
- Radeau – *Thunderer* (18 brass 24 pdrs)
- Gondolas – *Loyal Convert* (9 iron 9pdrs) and *Jersey* (7 iron 6pdrs)
- Gunboats – 24 with main body (1 brass 12pdr or howitzer); 4 with Advance Corps (using the unit's guns)
- Bateaux – 200+ (capable of carrying 40-50 men)

The *Washington*, *Lee* and *Jersey* were captured at Valcour Island the previous year.

Order of sailing: (1) Indians in birch canoes (20-30 warriors in each); (2) Brunswick jaegers and half Corps of Marksmen; (3) rest of German advance guard; (4) Prinz Ludwig Dragoons; (5) *Royal George* and *Inflexible* (towing pontoon bridge) and the brigs and sloops; (6) Powell's brigade (Hamilton's was at Sorel, guarding the transports and magazines); (7) Burgoyne (*Lady Maria*) with Phillips and Riedesel in their own pinnaces; (8) the brigades of Specht and Gall.

JULY 7 1777
HUBBARDTON

BRITISH

Brig Gen Simon Fraser	(850 men)
Corps of Marksmen – Capt Alexander Fraser (34th Foot)	2 / 48
Loyalists and Indians – Lt Col John Peters	c.100 all ranks
24th Foot – Maj Robert Grant (two companies)	7 / 92
Grenadier Battalion – Maj John Acland, MP (20th Foot)	16 / 300
(companies from 9th, 20th, 29th, 34th and 62nd Foot)	
Light Battalion – Maj Alexander Lindsay (53rd Foot)	16 / 290
(companies from 29th, 34th, 47th, 53rd and 62nd Foot)	

GERMANS

Maj Gen Frederick von Riedesel	(180 men)
Pickets – Capt Maximillian Schottelius (Gren/Light Battalions)	c.80 all ranks
Jaegers – Capt Carl von Geyso (Geisau)	c.100 all ranks

Not engaged

Grenadier Battalion – Maj Otto von Mengen	17 / 477 (less 40)
Light Battalion – Maj Ferdinand von Barner	22 / 560 (less 40)

Casualties

British – 50 killed, 134 wounded, 0 Missing
Germans – 10 killed, 14 wounded, 0 missing

AUGUST 16 1777
BENNINGTON

Lt Col Baum (723 all ranks, two 3pdrs)	Strength	Losses
Prinz Ludwig Dragoons		
(Maj Maiborn – HQ and three troops)	16 / 205	16 / 199
Grenadier Battalion (Lt Burghoff)	1 / 24	1 / 23
Light Battalion (Capt Thomas)	2 / 57	2 / 55
Line Infantry detachment (Ensign Andrea)	1 / 37	1 / 37
(Regt von Riedesel – 1 / 19, Regt von Rhetz – 0 / 2; Regt von Specht – 0 / 16)		
Hesse-Hanau Artillery (Lt Bach)	1 / 13	1 / 13
Queen's Loyal Rangers (Lt Col Peters)	150+	120+
Corps of Marksmen (Capt Fraser)	2 / 48	1 / 43
Local Loyalists (Lt Col Pfister, Capt Covel)	150+	120+
Canadians (?)	56	all
Indians (Capt de Lanaudière, Capt Campbell)	100+	unknown

Casualties

700+ killed or captured (NB: servants ignored in both columns)
Only nine Germans and six British (including Fraser) escaped

Lt Col Breymann (644 all ranks, two 6pdrs)	Strength	Losses
Grenadier Battalion	10 / 323	6 / 114
Light Battalion	11 / 277	6 / 96
Hesse-Hanau Artillery	1 / 20	1 / 8

Casualties

231 (2 officers / 18 other ranks killed, 6 / 65 wounded, 5 / 137 'missing').

Crown Point, New York
Ten miles north of Fort Ticonderoga, the site was first fortified in 1731, but the main works were begun (though never completed) in 1759. Though dilapidated, it became a forward supply base for the American invasion of Canada and a hospital and rallying point following their retreat. It was briefly recaptured by Carleton. In June 1777, it was being used by St Clair's ranger units, until they were forced to withdraw by the overwhelming numbers of Indians of Fraser's Advance Corps. Attempts to restore the fort have been thwarted by damage to the ground and buildings caused by the extremes of temperatures in summer and winter. (Author's photograph)

THE ARMY OF BRIG GEN BARRY ST LEGER
Brig Gen Barry St Leger, 34th Foot

Staff: Adjutants (Capt Ancrum, Lt Crofts)
                Quarter Master Gen (Lt Lundy)
                Aides de Camp (Lt Hamilton, Ensign Sturgis)

Royal Artillery – Lt Glennie	1 / 41[1]
(Two 6pdrs, two 3pdrs, four royal mortars)	
8th Foot – Capt Lernoult	6 / 118
34th Foot – (?)	6 / 134
Jaeger Company [Hesse-Hanau] – Lt Hildebrandt [2]	80 all ranks
(King's) Royal Regiment of New York – Col Sir John Johnson [3]	380 all ranks
Rangers [4] – Col John Butler	72 all ranks
Canadian militia	50 all ranks
Batteaux-men	400 (approx)
Iroquois – Chief Thayendanegea (aka Joseph Brant)	800 (approx) [5]

Total   2,000 (approx)

Footnotes

1 Includes one corporal and 20 men from the 8th and 34th Foot, and Johnson's Loyalists.
2 Some historians erroneously credit the jaegers with 388 officers and men; in fact, much of the unit was delayed en route to Canada, and the number given here is from documents captured during the siege.
3 This unit (also called 'Johnson's Royal Greens' or 'Royal Yorkers') is usually credited with 133 all ranks, most likely from a clerical error in London. A captured orderly book and the number of officers present implies the presence of several companies.
4 Often wrongly called 'Butler's Rangers' – a unit not formed until December 1777.
5 Mainly Mohawks, Senecas, and Cayugas; 800 appears the most realistic total for actual operations.

THE ARMY OF LT GEN SIR HENRY CLINTON [1]   (c. 3,500)
Lt Gen Sir Henry Clinton

Advance Guard: Lt Col Campbell, 52nd Foot	
52nd Foot (Lt Col Mungo Campbell)	240 all ranks
57th Foot (Lt Col John Campbell)	240 all ranks
Loyal Americans (Col Beverley Robinson)	200 all ranks
New York Volunteers (Maj Alexander Grant)	200 all ranks
Von Emmerich's Chasseurs (one company)	70 all ranks

Main body: Maj Gen The Hon. John Vaughan

Flank battalion (flank companies of 7th and 26th Foot	200 all ranks
26th Foot (Lt Col the Hon. Charles Stuart)	20 / 318
63rd Foot (Lt Col James Paterson)	19 / 429
71st Foot (one company)	3 / 60
17th Light Dragoons (one dismounted troop)	1 / 24
1st Anspach-Bayreuth Regiment, grenadier company	5 / 105

Rearguard: Maj Gen William Tryon (Royal Governor of New York)

7th Foot (Lt Col Alured Clarke)	18 / 287
Regiment von Trmbach [Hesse Kassel] (Col Carl von Bischhausen)	20 / 425
King's American Regiment (Lt Col Edmund Fanning)	22 / 310
King's Orange Rangers (Lt Col John Bayard)	
	13 / 156

Footnote

1 The 45th Foot (Maj William Gardiner) 19 / 372, Hessian Grenadier Battalion No.4 (Lt Col Johann von Koehler) 15 / 400, and 2nd Anspach-Bayreuth Regiment (Col August Voit von Salzburg) 28 / 511, later joined the column, with provisions for 5,000 men for six months, but saw no action.

AMERICAN FORCES

JUNE / JULY 1777
THE NORTHERN ARMY
Maj Gen Arthur St. Clair

Staff (Lt Col Udney Hay, Maj Isaac Dunn, Maj Henry Livingston)	
Engineer (Col Taddeus Kosciuszko)	
Artillery (Maj Ebenezer Stevens)	c.200 [1]
Artificers (Col Jeduthan Baldwin)	9 / 132 (3)
Whitcomb's Rangers	6 / 44 (2)
Lee's Rangers	3 / 27 (0)

Brig Gen Enoch Poor [2]

1st New Hampshire (Col Joseph Cilley)	30 / 432 (115)
2nd New Hampshire (Col Nathan Hale)	33 / 404 (89)
3rd New Hampshire (Col Alexander Scammel)	25 / 403 (139)

Brig Gen John Paterson

10th Massachusetts (Col Thomas Marshall)	25 / 323 (130)
11th Massachusetts (Col Ebenezer Francis)	36 / 463 (105)
12th Massachusetts (Col Samuel Brewer)	29 / 283 (49)
14th Massachusetts (Col Gamaliel Bradford)	26 / 370 (51)

Brig Gen Matthias de Rochefermoy

Additional Continental Regiment (Col Seth Warner)	27 / 207 (49)
8th Massachusetts (Col Michael Jackson)	6 / 99 (29)
New Hampshire Militia (Col Pierce Long)	29 / 173 (25)
Massachusetts Militia (Col ? Leonard)	26 / 312 (24)
Massachusetts Militia (Col ? Wells)	24 / 347 (68)

Footnotes

1 Figures indicate the number of officers and men present and fit for duty, with (in brackets) the total of sick (present and absent), on command (including 200 men training as gunners), and those on furlough.
2 The actual make-up of each brigade is somewhat speculative.

Fort Ticonderoga from the 'horseshoe battery' on Mount Independence. **The fort is about a half-mile away and the narrows are some 400 yards wide. Prior to the Declaration of Independence, Mount Independence was known as Rattlesnake Hill (Mount Defiance was Sugar Loaf Hill). The decision to fortify the Vermont side of the lake was prompted by its commanding views to the north and its fresh water supply (both of which Fort Ticonderoga lacked). (Author's photograph)**

JULY 7 1777
HUBBARDTON

Rearguard: Col Ebenezer Francis (1,300 all ranks)

Detachments[1] (Col Francis)	500
Additional Continental Regiment (Col Warner)	300[2]
2nd New Hampshire (Col Hale)	250
Stragglers, etc.	250

Not engaged

Massachusetts Militia (Col Leonard)	300
Massachusetts Militia (Col Wells)	350

Casualties
41 killed, 96 wounded, 234 captured

Footnotes

1 The rearguard comprised detachments of the 1st, 2nd, and 3rd New Hampshire, 11th Massachusetts (Francis's own regiment), and Warner's regiment (probably two companies of each).
2 Included detached company of the 2nd New Hampshire (Capt Carr's) and about 100 militia.

JULY / AUGUST 1777
THE NORTHERN ARMY
Maj Gen Philip Schuyler[1]

Brig Gen John Nixon
1,102 all ranks fit and present, 363 sick, 86 'on command', 3 on leave
Brig Gen Matthias De Rochefermoy
689 all ranks fit and present, 135 sick, 64 'on command', 3 on leave
Brig Gen Enoch Poor
698 all ranks fit and present, 168 sick, 90 'on command', 1 on leave
Brig Gen John Paterson
716 all ranks fit and present, 157 sick, 82 'on command', 2 on leave
Brig Gen Ebenezer Learned
679 all ranks fit and present, 106 sick, 45 'on command', 4 on leave

Total – 5,193[2]
(3,884 all ranks fit and present, 929 sick, 367 'on command', 13 on leave)

Footnotes

1 Figures are from the returns of July 26 – it has not been possible to identify the regiments in each brigade, but presumably the organisation was somewhere between the orders of battle of the Northern Army under St Clair and Gates.
2 There are no figures for the militia, but probably between 1,000 and 1,500 fit and present.

AUGUST 16 1777
BENNINGTON

Brig Gen John Stark (c.2,150)[1]

Col William Gregg (New Hampshire Militia)	200
Lt Col Moses Nichol (New Hampshire Militia)	350
Col Thomas Stickney (New Hampshire Militia)	150
Col David Hobart (New Hampshire Militia)	150
Reserve (New Hampshire Militia)	1,000
Col Samuel Herrick (Vermont Rangers/ Militia)	300

Col Seth Warner

Additional Continental Regiment (Lt Col Safford)	150
Vermont Rangers (?)	200

Casualties

30 killed, 40 wounded (Stark reported 14 killed, 42 wounded)

Footnote

1 Although most historians have Stark's force composed exclusively of New Hampshire and Vermont men, there were in fact several units from Massachusetts (including at least one – from Worcester – of mounted militia), although it has not been possible to identify them more precisely.

SEPTEMBER / OCTOBER 1777
THE NORTHERN ARMY[1]
Maj Gen Horatio Gates

Staff

Deputy Adjutant General – Lt Col James Wilkinson
Deputy Quartermaster General – Maj Morgan Lewis
Aides – Col UdnayHay, Maj John Armstrong, Col (militia) Van Vechten
Engineers – Col Taddeus Kosciuszko, Col Jeduthan Baldwin

Artillery

Independent Continental Artillery Battalion – Maj Ebenezer Stevens

September 7	c.400 all ranks serving 22 guns
October 16	498 all ranks fit and present, 42 sick, 8 'on command', 2 on leave, serving 40 guns

Cavalry

2nd Continental Light Dragoons, one troop – Lt Thomas Seymour
2nd Connecticut Light Horse – Maj Elijah Hyde

September 7	between 200 and 250 all ranks, of whom about 50 were Continentals
October 16	376 all ranks fit and present, 12 sick, 12 'on command', 1 on leave

LEFT WING
Maj Gen Benedict Arnold (to September 26)
Maj Gen Benjamin Lincoln (to October 8)

Advance Guard: Col Daniel Morgan
The riflemen had 374 all ranks fit and present out of 578 (the rest sick) at the start of September. The 300 Light Infantry were drawn from each brigade and are included among those 'on command'.

*Rifle Corps: 11th Virginia – Morgan
*Light Infantry – Maj Henry Dearborn (Lt Col from September 19)

Brig Gen Enoch Poor

September 7	1,292 all ranks fit and present, 356 sick, 153 'on command', 7 on leave
October 16	1,323 all ranks fit and present, 112 sick, 61 'on command', 11 on leave

The battlefield at Hubbardton, Vermont. **This view, looking east/south-east, shows the Castleton road (behind the white visitor center), with Pittsford Ridge in the background. (Author's photograph)**

*1st New Hampshire – Col Joseph Cilley
*2nd New Hampshire – Lt Col Winborn Adams (vice Hale)
*3rd New Hampshire – Col Alexander Scammel
*2nd New York – Col Philip van Cortlandt
*4th New York – Col Henry Livingston
*1st Regiment (Connecticut Militia) – Col Thaddeus Cook (arrived September 12)
*2nd Regiment (Connecticut Militia) – Col Jonathan Lattimore (arrived September 12)

Brig Gen Ebenezer Learned

September 7   1,393 all ranks fit and present, 229 sick, 54 'on command', 2 on leave
October 16   1,801 all ranks fit and present, 108 sick, 44 'on command', 8 on leave.

*2nd Massachusetts – Col John Bailey
*8th Massachusetts – Lt Col John Brooks (vice Jackson)
*9th Massachusetts – Col James Wesson
*1st Canadian Regiment – Col James Livingston
Two regiments of New Hampshire militia – arrived after October 7

RIGHT WING
Maj Gen Benjamin Lincoln (to September 26)

Brig Gen John Glover

September 7   1,555 all ranks fit and present, 397 sick, 233 'on command', 2 on leave
October 16   2,091 all ranks fit and present, 1,163 sick, 86 'on command', 23 on leave

1st Massachusetts – Col Joseph Vose
4th Massachusetts – Col William Shepard
13th Massachusetts – Col Edward Wigglesworth
15th Massachusetts – Col Timothy Bigelow (4 companies – arrived October 4)
2nd Albany County Regiment (New York militia) – Col Abraham Wemple
17th Albany County Regiment (New York Militia) – Col William Whiting
Dutchess and Ulster County Regiment (New York Militia) – Col Morris Graham

Brig Gen John Nixon

September 7   1,270 all ranks fit and present, 307 sick, 167 'on command', 4 on leave
October 16   1,545 all ranks fit and present, 142 sick, 73 'on command', 9 on leave

3rd Massachusetts – Col John Greaton
5th Massachusetts – Col Rufus Putnam
6th Massachusetts – Col Thomas Nixon
7th Massachusetts – Col Ichabod Alden
One regiment of Massachusetts militia (arrived after September 19)

Brig Gen John Paterson

September 7   1,243 all ranks fit and present, 229 sick, 54 'on command', 2 on leave
October 16   1,801 all ranks fit and present, 108 sick, 44 'on command', 8 on leave.

*10th Massachusetts – Col Thomas Marshall

11th Massachusetts – Lt Col Benjamin Tupper (vice Francis)

12th Massachusetts – Col Samuel Brewer

14th Massachusetts – Col Gamaliel Bradford

*1st South Berkshire Regiment (Massachusetts militia – arrived after September 19)

3rd York Regiment (Massachusetts militia – arrived after September 19)

Col Seth Warner
October 16   1,833 all ranks fit and present, 178 sick, 68 'on command',
                32 on leave.
+Warner's Continental Regiment (Green Mountain Boys)
+Five regiments of Massachusetts militia

Brig Gen Abraham Ten Broeck
October 16   1,260 all ranks fit and present, 119 sick, 553 'on
                command', 14 on leave.
#Ten Albany County regiments (New York militia)
(Probably: 1st, 3rd, 4th, 5th, 6th, 7th, 8th, 9th, 10th, 11th, 12th, 13th, 14th, 16th)

Brig Gen John Fellows
October 16   497 all ranks fit and present (incl. 118 officers), 57 sick,
                1,019 'on command'
Unknown number of regiments of Massachusetts militia

INDEPENDENT COMMANDS

Brig Gen John Stark
October 16
497 all ranks fit and present (incl. 128 officers), 57 sick, 1,019 'on command',
7 on leave.
+Unknown number of regiments of New Hampshire militia

Brig Gen William Whipple
October 16
388 all ranks fit and present (incl. 123 officers), 39 sick, 897 'on command',
27 on leave.
+Unknown number of regiments of New Hampshire militia

Brig Gen Jacob Bailey
October 16
1,147 all ranks fit and present, 53 sick, 48 'on command', 13 on leave.
+Unknown number of regiments of Vermont militia

Brig Gen James Brickett
October 16
1,019 all ranks fit and present, 58 sick, 31 'on command', 4 on leave.
Unknown number of regiments of Massachusetts militia

Brig Gen Oliver Wolcott
October 16
1,092 all ranks fit and present, 61 sick, 38 'on command', 7 on leave.
Unknown number of regiments of Connecticut militia

Fort Stanwix (Schuyler), viewed from the south-west. **Built in 1758 (at a cost of $266,000), the fort saw little action in the French and Indian Wars, and after 1760 fell into disrepair. Its dimensions were: perimeter 1,450 feet; stockade 14 feet high; moat 14 feet deep, 40 feet wide at the top, 16 feet at the bottom; walls 17 feet above the parade ground. The moat had a 'covered way' guarded by a row of vertical pickets; barracks, offices, and storerooms were built into the walls and 'bomb-proof' magazines were set into the south-west bastion. (Author's photograph)**

Footnotes

1 While even the British took their regimental book-keeping reasonably seriously, the inexperience and indolence of many Continental brigade majors and adjutants conspired to make life difficult for their superiors. When records were kept, their provenance often made them doubtful assets – a return for Nixon's brigade on July 12 suggested 853 all ranks present and fit for duty, with 123 sick also present, whereas the real figures were 575 and 11. Ironically, equivalent post-holders in militia units probably had more experience – if not necessarily greater competence – in such duties (although few militiamen needed reminding when pay or food were due, or when a period of enlistment had expired). One of Schuyler's returns (July 26) contained the note: '(T)he present Ignorance of the Brigade Majors, and the [illegible] of the Adjutants, render it impossible for me to form Accurate or Correct Returns'.

On September 7, Gates reported 6,043 Continental infantry (492 regimental officers and 782 NCOs to just 4,688 rank and file) present, excluding riflemen. Another 780 other ranks were 'on command' – about half with Dearborn, the rest holding isolated posts in the rear – and 1,458 other ranks were sick, of whom 655 were present and 803 'absent' (i.e. in hospital).

On October 16, Gates informed Burgoyne he had 16,056 infantry, 376 cavalry and 498 artillerymen, with over 40 guns (including the independent brigades of militia, whose numbers fluctuated daily as men joined or went home). Gates probably had little idea how many militia were blocking Burgoyne's way – but then Burgoyne had even less.

2 In the breakdown that follows (**Left Wing**, **Right Wing**, and **Independent Commands**);
* indicates unit fought in both September 19 and October 7 actions
# indicates unit fought in October 7 action only
+ indicates brigade contains units which fought at Bennington

BURGOYNE MOVES SOUTH

Burgoyne arrived back in Canada on May 6, bearing a letter from Germain dated March 26, approving his plan and ordering Carleton (whom it liberally insulted for his 'failure' the previous year) to support him. The plan required Carleton to hold Canada with 3,700 men (later reduced to 3,000), while Burgoyne with 8,000 (later increased to 10,000) moved down Lake Champlain, and St Leger with 2,000 headed along the Mohawk to converge on Albany. There they would await the arrival of Howe. Germain had also approved Howe's proposal to attack Philadelphia (offering him 5,500 reinforcements), but stressed that Howe must return in time to aid Burgoyne. For some reason, Howe received a copy of Burgoyne's plan but no directions as to his own role: in fact, Howe had already written to Carleton (on April 5), warning him that any army leaving Canada should not rely on him, but could – if necessary – be supported by Clinton in New York City.

Despite bad weather, troops and shipping assembled at St John's throughout May. On Friday June 13, the Royal Standard was unfurled aboard *Thunderer* and the fleet set sail. On June 20, Burgoyne visited the

Major General Sir Guy Carleton (1724-1808). **A former Foot Guards officer, Carleton was well-liked by the Canadians. Aware of Burgoyne's intrigues in London and inexperience of North America, Carleton anticipated his needs. He repaired the Lake Champlain fleet, established depots at Montreal, Sorel and Chambly, concentrated his best troops at St John's, alerted the Indian Departments and invoked the *corvée* in an attempt to raise the 1,000 warriors, 2,000 workmen and 1,000 boatmen Burgoyne wanted. (National Archives of Canada, C-2833)**

LEFT *Fort Ticonderoga from Lake Champlain, by J. Hunter.* **These views show Fraser's Advance Corps landing at Three Mile Point: note the gun-boats with their 12pdrs in the bows and the various bateaux. The men standing in the foreground (above) are believed to depict Alexander Fraser's corps of marksmen. (National Archives of Canada, C-1524 and C-1525)**

BURGOYNE'S PLAN: SPRING 1777

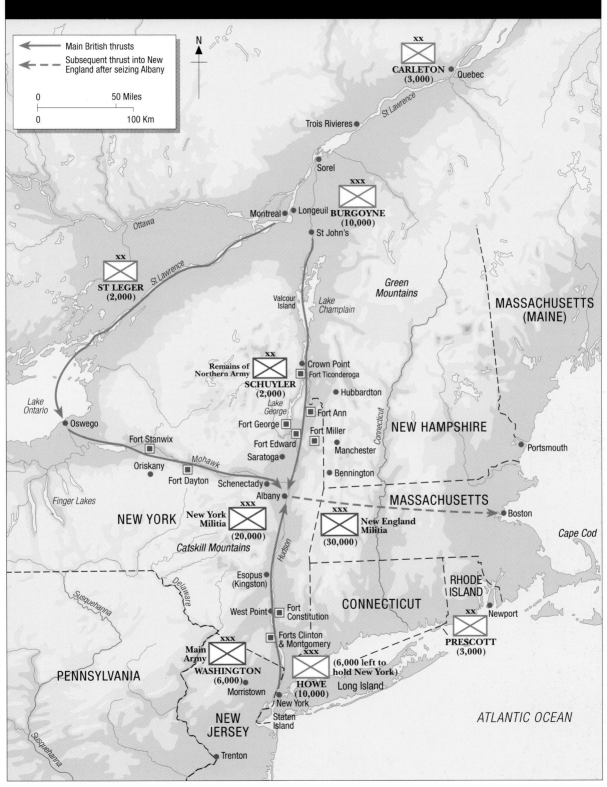

Legend:
- Main British thrusts
- Subsequent thrust into New England after seizing Albany

0 — 50 Miles
0 — 100 Km

N

CARLETON (3,000) — Quebec

Trois Rivieres — St Lawrence

Sorel

BURGOYNE (10,000)

Montreal ● Longueuil

St John's

Ottawa

ST LEGER (2,000)

St Lawrence

Valcour Island

Lake Champlain

Green Mountains

MASSACHUSETTS (MAINE)

Lake Ontario

Oswego

Fort Stanwix

Oriskany

Mohawk

Fort Dayton

Schenectady

Finger Lakes

Remains of Northern Army SCHUYLER (2,000)

Crown Point
Fort Ticonderoga

Hubbardton

Lake George

Fort Ann

Fort George

Fort Miller

Fort Edward

Saratoga

Manchester

Bennington

Connecticut

NEW HAMPSHIRE

Portsmouth

Albany

NEW YORK

New York Militia (20,000)

Catskill Mountains

Hudson

New England Militia (30,000)

MASSACHUSETTS

Boston

Cape Cod

Susquehanna

Delaware

Esopus (Kingston)

West Point — Fort Constitution

Forts Clinton & Montgomery

Main Army WASHINGTON (6,000)

Morristown

HOWE (10,000)

(6,000 left to hold New York)

Long Island

CONNECTICUT

RHODE ISLAND

Newport

PRESCOTT (3,000)

PENNSYLVANIA

New York

Staten Island

NEW JERSEY

Trenton

Susquehanna

ATLANTIC OCEAN

Advance Corps under Brigadier General Simon Fraser at the Bouquet River, five miles ahead of the main body and 30 miles from Crown Point. Here, Burgoyne issued a proclamation ordering the populace to either join him or remain neutral – if anyone opposed him, he would unleash the Indians with a clear conscience. He offered the Indians higher prices for live prisoners, to discourage scalping, and exhorted them to differentiate between friend and foe, soldier and civilian, and to spare the wounded. (Subsequently, whigs on both sides of the Atlantic lampooned his speeches, and even his own officers felt that using Indians was a mistake.)

On June 25, the Advance Corps landed, unopposed, at Crown Point and next day the main force began to arrive. Violent rainstorms, which delayed the advance for three days, gave way to intense, muggy heat and clouds of blackflies, but on June 30, each man received eight days' rations before being read a general order that concluded: 'This army must not retreat'. The next day, the troops rowed down the lake, the British hugging the west bank, the Germans the east, and camped at Three Mile Point.

First encounter – Fort Ticonderoga

After capturing Fort Ticonderoga in 1775, the Americans had tried to repair the existing defenses and had begun to fortify Mount Independence. However, they had faced three problems: first, Fort Ticonderoga faced the wrong way, having been built to stop a British advance from the south; second, the extended defenses needed a

Mount Defiance and Fort Ticonderoga from Mount Independence. **The view west across Lake Champlain, from the site of the dock where Long and his party embarked for Skenesboro. In July 1776, Schuyler's deputy adjutant general, Lieutenant Colonel John Trumbull, demonstrated that Mount Defiance could command the area by almost hitting its summit with balls fired from both Fort Ticonderoga and Mount Independence. (Author's photograph)**

RIGHT *Fort Ticonderoga from Fort Independence, by Lt H. Rudyard.* **A contemporary watercolor by one of Burgoyne's engineer officers, showing clearly the piers of the bridge (which the British had demolished to allow vessels to pass), the *Inflexible* (far left) and Mount Hope behind the fort. (Fort Ticonderoga Museum)**

LEFT *Fort Ticonderoga and Fort Independence from Mount Defiance.* **Mount Independence is straight ahead and Fort Ticonderoga is just visible to the left of the 'narrows' (Ticonderoga means 'the place where the lake shuts itself') just left of center. Lake George is behind the viewer and the view shows how the fort controlled the southern approaches to its junction with Lake Champlain. Winters were so cold that St Clair's predecessor, Anthony Wayne, was chosen for his physical fitness! Even he thought it 'the last part of the world that God made' and that it had been 'finished in the dark'. (Author's photograph)**

garrison of 10,000 – over three times their strength in June 1777; and third, Mount Defiance (800 feet high) dominated both positions – something successive commanders had either ignored or had had neither the time nor the manpower to remedy. The arrival in February 1777 of the engineer Colonel Jeduthan Baldwin had finally injected some urgency into the situation. He designed blockhouses to guard the Lake George portage and Mount Hope, and once the thaw had begun, commenced work on a 12-foot-wide bridge between the forts and a heavy log boom across the 400-yard narrows.

On June 12, St Clair arrived to take over command, his predecessor Anthony Wayne, having departed in April. On June 19, with another six weeks' work needed to complete Fort Independence, St Clair met with Schuyler and his brigadiers and agreed that they should try to defend both banks, but should abandon the New York side first if necessary, and that if the enemy arrived in strength, the garrison should withdraw to avoid capture.

On July 2, Burgoyne sent Simon Fraser to seize Mount Hope. St Clair withdrew its garrison under cover of a sortie from Fort Ticonderoga, and when a captured British skirmisher provided a detailed breakdown of Burgoyne's army, it confirmed St Clair's hope that Burgoyne would risk an assault, after which he could abandon the fort with honor. However, on July 4, the British engineer Lieutenant Twiss dashed this hope by pronouncing it possible to haul guns up Mount Defiance: led by Phillips, the gunners spent July 5 doing just that. Unfortunately, either Indian campfires or a careless shot at an enemy vessel on the lake warned St Clair of the threat while the British were still awaiting Riedesel's arrival at Fort Independence. St Clair's brigadiers agreed, though not without argument, that evacuation was the only option.

Despite a full moon, the British remained unaware of proceedings (even when two huts caught fire, it was assumed to be a ruse). The women, the sick, and all the supplies that could be saved were put onto vessels at Mount Independence and sent to Skenesboro, with 600 troops under Colonel Long. St Clair's remaining 2,500 men crossed to Mount Independence, then, after trying (and failing) to destroy the bridge, headed south on the military road to Castleton. However, on Mount Independence, the Frenchman de Rochefermoy had not only failed to

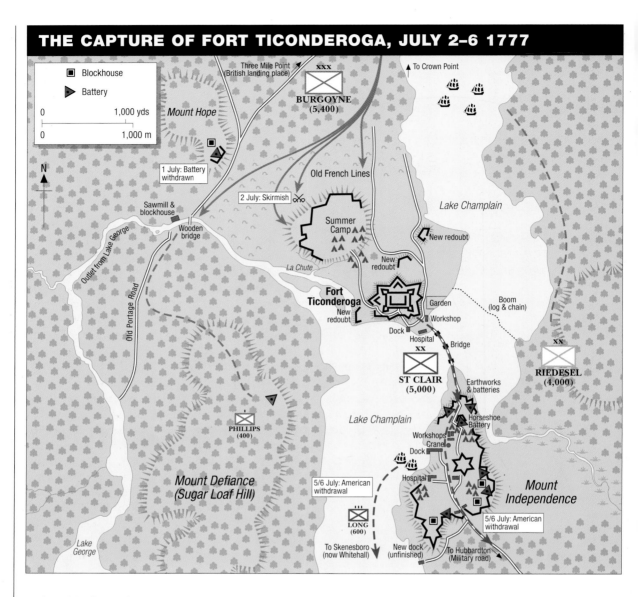

THE CAPTURE OF FORT TICONDEROGA, JULY 2–6 1777

Blockhouse

Battery

0   1,000 yds

0   1,000 m

N

Three Mile Point
(British landing place)

xxx
BURGOYNE
(5,400)

To Crown Point

Mount Hope

1 July: Battery
withdrawn

Sawmill &
blockhouse

Outlet from Lake George

Old Portage Road

Wooden
bridge

2 July: Skirmish

Old French Lines

Summer
Camp

La Chute

New
redoubt

Lake Champlain

New redoubt

**Fort
Ticonderoga**

New
redoubt

Garden

Workshop

Boom
(log & chain)

Dock

Hospital

Bridge

xx
ST CLAIR
(5,000)

Earthworks
& batteries

xx
RIEDESEL
(4,000)

Lake Champlain

Horseshoe
Battery

Workshops

Crane

Dock

▽
PHILLIPS
(400)

Hospital

**Mount Defiance
(Sugar Loaf Hill)**

*Mount
Independence*

5/6 July: American
withdrawal

5/6 July: American
withdrawal

**LONG
(600)**

*Lake
George*

To Skenesboro
(now Whitehall)

New dock
(unfinished)

To Hubbardton
(Military road)

order his brigade to leave, but had got drunk and set his own
headquarters alight. The smoke alerted Riedesel, but by the time his
advance guard arrived, the confusion had been sorted out and there was
only time to fire a few shots at the departing Americans. As dawn broke,
two deserters told Burgoyne of the withdrawal. He told Simon Fraser to
repair the bridge and rush his Advance Corps across, then ordered the
flotilla to break the boom and pursue Long. Within 30 minutes, the
vessels were through, and by 09.00 they were heading for Skenesboro.

Long reached Skenesboro around 13.00, having, from misplaced
confidence in the boom, ignored several opportunities to leave a
rearguard (in some places the lake was so narrow the vessels' yardarms
almost touched the cliffs). Around 15.00 – preceded by gunboats, the
Royal George, and the *Inflexible* – Powell's brigade arrived at Skenesboro
and landed between South Bay and Wood Creek, setting three enemy
vessels alight and capturing two others. Some of Long's men withdrew
into a blockhouse, which they later burned, along with Colonel Skene's

Mill and blockhouse at Skenesboro.
Philip Skene had received a grant of 34,000 acres (later increased to 60,000 by purchase) at the southern end of Lake Champlain for his service in the French and Indian Wars. By 1775, when he was also appointed governor of Crown Point and Fort Ticonderoga, he had developed a small empire, based on Skenesboro (now Whitehall), with sawmills, iron foundries, and shipyards. Arrested and imprisoned in Connecticut, on his release he served with Howe and then became Burgoyne's principal 'local' advisor – a post that caused some resentment among other Loyalists, undoubtedly contributing to the idea that he directed Burgoyne's movements to his own advantage. (Fort Ticonderoga Museum)

ironworks, before fleeing south to Fort Ann pursued by 190 men of the 9th, under Lieutenant Colonel Hill. Although delayed by bad roads, broken bridges, and the fires that spread from Skenesboro to the surrounding woods, by nightfall Hill had captured the boats with the women and sick and made camp a mile from Fort Ann.

The action at Hubbardton

Simon Fraser, with half his Advance Corps, had left Mount Independence around 04.00, followed by Riedesel with Breymann's command. Riedesel caught up with Fraser around 16.00 and in an amicable, if slightly awkward, meeting (Riedesel was technically Fraser's superior, but respected the latter's experience in North America) they agreed that Fraser would continue for three miles, despite his men not having eaten all day, and that both groups would resume at 03.00 on July 7. As Fraser arrived at Lacey's Camp (which the Americans had abandoned only an hour earlier), captured stragglers warned that the rearguard comprised picked men under a competent officer – Colonel Ebenezer Francis.

In the oppressive heat, it had taken St Clair most of July 6 to reach Hubbardton, where the military road met the main road to Crown Point. Informed (wrongly) that 500 Loyalists and Indians had already passed by, he sent his main body on to Castleton, six miles further, leaving Colonel Nathan Hale to round up stragglers and Colonel Seth Warner to lead Francis's rearguard back to Castleton. When Francis arrived around 16.00, the three colonels decided to ignore Warner's orders and stay there that night (either because of the state of the men, or in the belief that they could outmarch their enemies). However, they failed to post enough pickets or move Hale's group away from the most advanced and vulnerable part of the line (possibly for the same reasons).

During the night, Indians located the Americans and the British Captain Fraser's Marksmen moved off before dawn. They were led by Peters' corps, followed by Fraser with two companies of the 24th and half of the light infantry and grenadier battalions (under majors the Earl of Balcarres and Acland respectively). Around 04.30 the Indians overwhelmed a picket: halting on the saddle above Sucker Brook, Simon Fraser could see Hale's campfires and sent on the 24th. The companies guarding the brook opened fire, causing 21 casualties and killing the 24th's commander, Major Grant. The British swept on, turning left up the hill toward Francis, who had just heard from St Clair of the disaster at Skenesboro.

As the Light infantry and 24th closed on the Castleton road, Fraser ordered Acland to climb Zion Hill, which commanded the road, and sent word to Riedesel to hurry forward. Francis decided to turn Fraser's left, drive him back across the military road and sever Fraser's line of communication; Francis advanced to the crest of the ridge (now Monument Hill) and fired into the Light infantry, forcing them back. Further south, the grenadiers had reached Zion Hill and left two companies to guard the woods at its base. They were approached by 60

35

MOUNT INDEPENDENCE, JULY 6 1777
As St Clair's garrison abandoned Fort Ticonderoga and Mount Independence on the night of July 5, they left behind a 'forlorn hope' of four gunners in the main shore battery covering the bridge of boats linking the two posts. Any British attempt to pursue the Ticonderoga garrison should have resulted in a massacre and the destruction of the bridge: unfortunately the gunners discovered a cask of Madeira, became drunk and were surprised in the early hours by a party of Indians.

Americans with 'clubbed' muskets (a sign of surrender) who suddenly reversed arms and fired from ten yards, causing heavy loss and wounding Acland in the thigh. As the surviving British pursued them, giving no quarter, the other three grenadier companies seized the road, forcing Warner back to the Selleck farm. In the center, the British again climbed the hill, overlapping Francis's left: he counter-attacked, and in the close fighting, had his right arm shattered, while Balcarres was wounded twice.

Meanwhile, Riedesel was urging his men towards the firing and soon reached the saddle, from where Fraser had seen the camp fires. Sending Breymann orders to hurry up, he called to his men to start singing: the sound caused apprehension among friend and foe alike. With his jaegers bolstering the British left, the infantry detachment encircled the American right, just as Fraser ordered Balcarres (who now had ten bullet holes in his coat) to take the ridge at bayonet point. The Americans fell back in disorder across the Castleton road, and Francis was killed trying to rally them behind a high log fence. As Balcarres climbed the hill and joined the jaegers for another attack, the Americans broke and fled over Pittsford Ridge into New Hampshire, leaving Hale and over 200 stragglers in British hands.

In Castleton, St Clair heard the firing. He sent two aides to locate the two militia regiments encamped between there and Hubbardton and use them to reinforce Francis, while he tried, in vain, to lead his own men back. As St Clair heard the musketry die away, he was passed by the militia (who had refused to advance) and an hour later his aides, who had ridden on to Hubbardton alone, returned to report that the battle was over. Wearily, he ordered his men to head for Rutland, to avoid any British pursuit.

The British were too exhausted to pursue Warner or St Clair's main body, and a rainstorm prevented them from doing anything more than collect the injured and bury the dead. When Breymann arrived the next day, the Germans marched to Skenesboro (according to Fraser, far more quickly than they had marched to his aid), leaving the British burdened with both sides' wounded and isolated in hostile country.

At Skenesboro on July 9 a 'deserter' informed Hill that there were 1,000 men in Fort Ann. On seeing how few men Hill had, and learning that Burgoyne was ten miles away, the 'deserter' returned to the fort and the 200-man garrison – reinforced by 400 New York militia – attacked Hill in a narrow defile in the woods. Fighting raged for several hours, and both sides' ammunition was running low, when Hill learned that the Americans had outflanked him by moving along a small creek. He withdrew to a small ridge and all seemed lost until an Indian 'war whoop' was heard, at which the Americans promptly fled (it was actually a ruse by a lone British officer whose Indians had abandoned him). Hill then withdrew to Skenesboro, leaving an officer, 15 men (all wounded), and his surgeon in American hands and temporarily abandoning his uncaptured wounded, whom he rescued on July 16 (except for three who died, almost all had recovered by the time they were back at Skenesboro). American losses were, according to one report, around 200 and they were forced to burn Fort Ann and fall back 30 miles. In ten days, Burgoyne had captured Fort Ticonderoga, 200 vessels, 100 cannon,

Brigadier General Simon Fraser (1729-77), attributed to J. Smart. **One of many officers of this name in the British Army in the 18th century, Fraser served in the 78th Foot (Fraser's Highlanders) under Wolfe, and as a staff officer in Germany, before becoming major of the 24th Foot in 1762, and later its lieutenant colonel. The high standards of that unit led to his appointment to lead the Advance Corps, and his leadership and experience of North America proved vital at Hubbardton and Freeman's Farm. He was mortally wounded while rallying his men on October 7 and is buried in the Great Redoubt. Captain Alexander Fraser was his nephew. (New York Historical Society)**

FAR, RIGHT *Major John Dyke Acland (d. 1778), by Sir J. Reynolds.* **Acland joined the 33rd Foot in 1774, buying his way to major within two years. He had an action-packed campaign – a serious illness at Chambly, near-cremation in a tent fire, leg wounds and a spell in captivity. (Sir John Acland and N Toyne, LBIPP)**

RIGHT *Major Alexander Lindsay, 6th Earl of Balcarres (1752-1825), attributed to A. Naysmith.* **Shown here as lieutenant colonel of the 71st Foot, Balcarres joined the 53rd as a 15-year-old and purchased his way to major. He was wounded at Fort Ticonderoga and Hubbardton, and took over the withdrawal, after Fraser was shot. (Scottish National Portrait Gallery and the Earl of Crawford and Balcarres)**

BELOW *The battlefield at Hubbardton, Vermont.* **This view is to the north and north-west. The saddle (now Sargent's Hill) is at the far left, Sucker Brook runs behind the trees in the middle distance, and the stones mark the wall behind which Francis defended the ridge (now Monument Hill). The white house (far right) marks his second line, behind the high log fence. (Author's photograph)**

and masses of supplies, and forced the enemy all the way back to Fort Edward. Nothing, it seemed, could go wrong.

Burgoyne's road

Learning that Fort Ticonderoga was lost, Schuyler sent reinforcements to Fort Edward, but confessed to Washington that he had no idea where St Clair – or Burgoyne – were, and that he had little hope of halting the latter, given the state and numbers of troops he had available. (As the news spread, New Englanders became angry at the surrender of Fort Ticonderoga by the hated New Yorkers, even accusing Schuyler and St Clair of taking bribes.) When St Clair reached Fort Edward on July 12, having marched through Manchester and Bennington, Schuyler had 4,000 men – including 3,000 Continentals – but almost a third were sick and his only artillery (30 guns at Fort George) had no transport. With

PHASE 4: 07.30 TO 08.00
As Lindsay and Acland race south to cut the Castleton Road, Simon Fraser follows up the retreating companies, forcing Francis and Warner to occupy Monument Hill. After repulsing two attacks, the Americans withdraw across the road to a new position in farmland surrounded by a high log fence.

PHASE 5: 08.00 TO 08.45
As Lindsay captures Carr's flank guard and Hale's stragglers, and the grenadiers move up the steep slopes of Pittsford Ridge, Francis and Titcomb observe Fraser's exposed left flank and attack, but are themselves caught by Riedesel's men.

FRANCIS
(1,200)

PHASE 6: 08.45 TO 10.00
With Francis killed and the British Grenadiers and Riedesel's men threatening to outflank them, Warner and Titcomb order a retreat and the Americans withdraw eastwards over Pittsford Ridge in small groups.

ZION HILL

TO CASTLETON
AND SKENESBORO

SELLECK
CABIN

NORTH
BRETON
BROOK

TO PITTSFORD RIDGE

THE BATTLE OF HUBBARDTON
JULY 7 1777, 05.00–10.00

A view of the action taken from the north-east: the successive defensive positions adopted by Francis are shown, as is Fraser's approach from Fort Ticonderoga, and the British and German attacks.

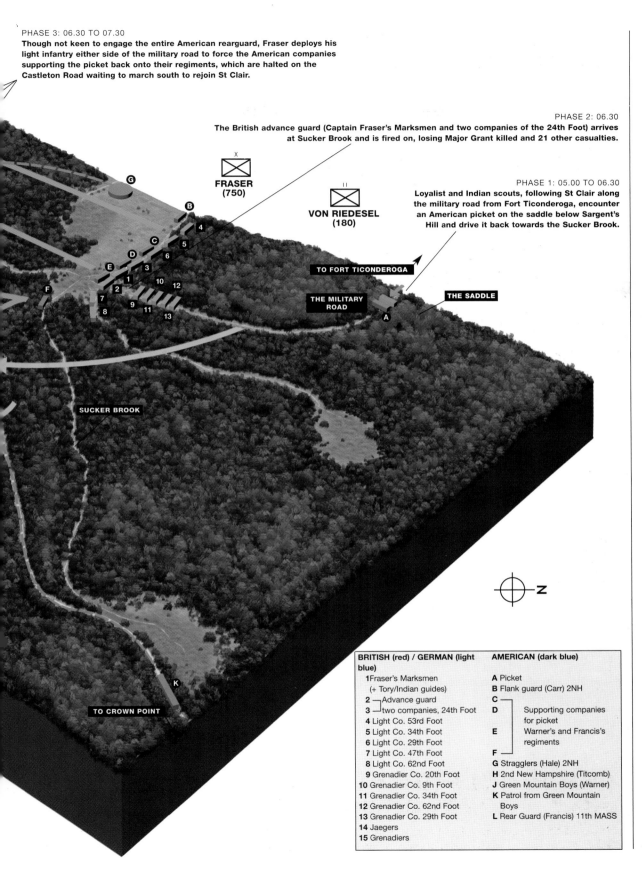

PHASE 3: 06.30 TO 07.30
Though not keen to engage the entire American rearguard, Fraser deploys his light infantry either side of the military road to force the American companies supporting the picket back onto their regiments, which are halted on the Castleton Road waiting to march south to rejoin St Clair.

PHASE 2: 06.30
The British advance guard (Captain Fraser's Marksmen and two companies of the 24th Foot) arrives at Sucker Brook and is fired on, losing Major Grant killed and 21 other casualties.

PHASE 1: 05.00 TO 06.30
Loyalist and Indian scouts, following St Clair along the military road from Fort Ticonderoga, encounter an American picket on the saddle below Sargent's Hill and drive it back towards the Sucker Brook.

FRASER (750)

VON RIEDESEL (180)

TO FORT TICONDEROGA

THE SADDLE

THE MILITARY ROAD

SUCKER BROOK

TO CROWN POINT

N

BRITISH (red) / GERMAN (light blue)	AMERICAN (dark blue)
1 Fraser's Marksmen (+ Tory/Indian guides)	**A** Picket
2 Advance guard	**B** Flank guard (Carr) 2NH
3 two companies, 24th Foot	**C**
4 Light Co. 53rd Foot	**D** Supporting companies for picket
5 Light Co. 34th Foot	**E** Warner's and Francis's regiments
6 Light Co. 29th Foot	**F**
7 Light Co. 47th Foot	**G** Stragglers (Hale) 2NH
8 Light Co. 62nd Foot	**H** 2nd New Hampshire (Titcomb)
9 Grenadier Co. 20th Foot	**J** Green Mountain Boys (Warner)
10 Grenadier Co. 9th Foot	**K** Patrol from Green Mountain Boys
11 Grenadier Co. 34th Foot	**L** Rear Guard (Francis) 11th MASS
12 Grenadier Co. 62nd Foot	
13 Grenadier Co. 29th Foot	
14 Jaegers	
15 Grenadiers	

Private, Braunschweig Jäger, by F. von Germann. **Often compared unfavorably with Morgan's corps, the jaegers (or jägers) fought well and were certainly better disciplined. Their shorter rifles ranged in caliber from 0.65 to 0.75 inches, allowing them to use standard musket balls, and took a 22-inch double-edged sword-bayonet. (Morgan's men, with non-standard rifles, had to make their own ammunition and could not fix a bayonet: Washington once proposed giving them seven-foot pikes, and eventually cut the number of rifles in his army.) Serving mainly in platoon-sized detachments, the jaegers were backed up by musketmen – grenadiers at Hubbardton, but more often the musketeer companies of von Barner's Light Battalion. Their use of a 'patched' ball produced a rate of fire comparable to musket-armed troops, but which often appeared slower because it was aimed. (Miriam and Ira D. Wallach Division, New York Public Library)**

his own men in equally bad shape, Washington could not march north himself, but ordered Nixon with 600 Continentals up from Peekskill. Everything would depend on how fast Burgoyne moved towards Albany.

On July 11, Burgoyne informed Howe of his success (in a letter which arrived eight days before Howe sailed for Philadelphia) and his tone merely confirmed Howe's view that Burgoyne could reach Albany unaided. However, Burgoyne was increasingly concerned at the length of his supply lines and their vulnerability to roving bands of militia and Continentals on his left. His choice of route to the Hudson would be vital, as his 'Thoughts' had anticipated. In them, he had analyzed both the land route from Skenesboro to Fort Edward – 23 miles of swamp which, he accurately predicted, the enemy would make even worse – or the Lake George route, which only required a ten-mile journey overland. Now he was there, he had insufficient vessels to carry his army and its supplies down Lake George; nor could he spare the 10 to 15 horses needed to drag each vessel over the Fort Ticonderoga portage or south from Lake George. Equally, he had only 180 light carts (each able to carry 800 pounds – a day's rations for 240 men), 30 ox-drawn wagons, and one third of the horses he had requested to keep 6,000 men supplied.

Possibly influenced by Skene (whose estates stood to benefit from a road link with Fort Edward), he decided to use both routes, sending his artillery by water and his main force by land. In reality, he had little choice, given his transportation problems; his real error appears to have been dallying too long in Castleton – ostensibly to suggest a strike into Connecticut – and Skenesboro, where he enjoyed Skene's hospitality while supplies were stockpiled. By the time Burgoyne left Skenesboro on July 24, Schuyler had turned the area into a desert, felling trees across roads (interlacing their branches to impede removal); damming brooks and digging trenches to remove drinking water and flood farmland; carrying off livestock; and burning crops. Nature added to his handiwork – July rains turned tracks into quagmires that bred swarms of insects. Occasional ambushes rounded off the discomfort of Burgoyne's artificers, as they took almost as many days per mile to build 23-miles of road to Fort Edward.

It took Burgoyne two days to march 14 miles to Fort Ann, where the main body halted while Simon Fraser advanced to Pine Plains, two miles from Fort Edward. On July 29, the main body came up and the whole force (minus many of the Indians who had left following Burgoyne's mishandling of the Jane McCrea affair[1]) marched to the Hudson. But Schuyler, having already abandoned Fort Edward – which was so dilapidated it was totally indefensible – and evacuated Fort George, withdrew across the Hudson to Saratoga, providing more ammunition for his detractors, but once again saving his army.

Footnote

1 Jane McCrea's death – perhaps the most enduring myth of the campaign – was in all probability the result of poor shooting by an American patrol as Indians, under British officers, escorted her and a cousin of Simon Fraser to safety. Subsequent exhumation showed none of the injuries supposedly inflicted, but did provide three bullet holes. Given the oft-overlooked fact that her brother was a militia colonel, blaming the 'usual suspects' conveniently avoided awkward explanations back in Schuyler's camp. The claim that the incident roused the people against Burgoyne is nonsense; while his refusal to believe the Indians undoubtedly encouraged their mass departure, local newspapers hardly mention the story and the 'rallying cry' her death supposedly provided is just a fanciful piece of pseudo-history, retrospectively meeting the need for a 'Yankee Joan of Arc' so prophetically suggested by Thomas Paine some time earlier.

Colonel Peter Gansevoort (1749-1812), by G Stuart. **From a prominent Albany family, Gansevoort was commissioned into the 2nd New York Regiment as a major in 1775 and served under Montgomery in Canada. He then commanded at Fort George, before being promoted to colonel of the 3rd New York at the age of 28. It was at the head of this regiment that he distinguished himself at Fort Stanwix, for which he received the thanks of Congress. He ended the war as a major general of New York militia. (Munson-Williams-Proctor Institute Museum of Art, New York)**

Brigadier General Barry St Leger left Montreal on June 23 and two days later arrived at Oswego, where he was joined by Sir John Johnson and Joseph Brant with almost 1,000 Iroquois. The following day, they crossed Lake Oneida and, screened by Brant's warriors, moved down Wood Creek, making a creditable ten miles per day, despite the terrain and frequent enemy obstacles. Their first objective was Fort Stanwix[1], guarding the portage between Wood Creek and the Mohawk River, which, despite good intelligence from Indian Department officers, St Leger believed was a ruin guarded by 60 men. In fact, it had been garrisoned since April by 550 men of the 3rd New York regiment under Colonel Peter Gansevoort, who had largely rebuilt it (despite a French engineer, Captain De Marquisie, wasting several weeks attempting to design an entirely new fort). By the end of July, only the east wall (which faced a 19-foot cliff and a swamp) had not been restored to some extent.

On August 2, St Leger's Advance Guard, which had been sent ahead to intercept an expected supply convoy, arrived just too late to stop 200 men escorting bateaux filled with ammunition and six weeks' provisions into the fort. The next day, St Leger arrived with his main body and, seeing that his artillery was too weak in number and caliber, marched his entire force past the garrison, hoping to overawe them. In fact, the paucity of white troops and preponderance of Indians increased the American resolve, and Gansevoort refused St Leger's summons: later that day, a flag made from a soldier's shirt and a woman's petticoat was hoisted over the fort. As most of St Leger's force began building earthworks, clearing Wood Creek and cutting a 16-mile supply road through the woods, jaegers and Indian marksmen started sniping at the garrison, with some success. However, on the evening of August 5, St Leger heard that a relief force had left Fort Dayton the previous day and was within striking distance of his camp. Unwilling to risk a battle where the garrison might intervene, he sent Johnson and Brant, with 150 Loyalists and 400 Iroquois, to ambush the approaching column.

The Battle of Oriskany

Four regiments of Tryon County militia[2], each 200-strong, had been assembling since July 30, when their commander, Brigadier General Nicholas Herkimer, had called out all males between 16 and 60. Leaving Fort Dayton on August 4, they covered 12 miles before camping at Stirling Creek: next day, they crossed the Mohawk River and by nightfall they were eight miles from Fort Stanwix. However, Herkimer was concerned: his route was dangerous, and defeat would leave Gansevoort isolated and the valley defenseless. So he sent four men to warn Gansevoort of his approach and ask him to make a sortie: the four men's arrival was to be acknowledged by three cannon shots.

THE BATTLE OF ORISKANY, AUGUST 6 1777

Loyalists tried to penetrate the American lines by pretending to be reinforcements from Fort Stanwix, reversing their drab-faced green coats and marching towards their enemies as if on parade. Captain Gardenier of Visscher's regiment (the American rearguard) spotted the ruse when one of his men went out to greet these 'friends' and was promptly captured. Gardenier, armed only with a spontoon and sword, rushed forward and killed his man's captor: he then killed a second Loyalist and wounded a third, before three more knocked him down, two of them bayoneting him through the thighs. The third, a Lieutenant McDonald, went to bayonet him in the chest, but Gardenier caught the bayonet with his left hand, which cut him badly, but brought MacDonald down on top of him. As a militiaman distracted the other two attackers, Gardenier grabbed his spontoon and killed McDonald with a single thrust, then shouted, 'They are not our men – they are the enemy! Fire away!'

PHASE 4: 17.30 TO 18.00
Soon after Breymann's column crosses St Luke's bridge, he meets
survivors of Baum's command and sees their pursuers occupying
the high ground on his left.

TO SAN COICK'S MILL
AND CAMBRIDGE

LITTLE WHITE CREEK

BREYMANN
(650)

PHASE 6: 18.00 TO 20.00
After driving back the nearest American forces,
Breymann's column is halted by reinforcements brought up
by Stark and Warner. Suffering heavy casualties and running
short of ammunition, Breymann is forced to retreat to Cambridge
and only nightfall prevents his command suffering the same fate
as that of Baum.

PHASE 5: 17.30 TO 18.00
Warner has reached the battlefield and follows Stark westwards to
oppose Breymann, as the prisoners (J) are marched off towards
Bennington.

WARNER
(350)

PHASE 3: 15.00 TO 17.00
The Tory Redoubt and cabins and the baggage park are quickly overrun, leaving the dragoons in the main redoubt
completely isolated. After fierce fighting, they run out of ammunition and try to charge through the encircling
cordon – the vast majority being killed or captured in the process.

THE BATTLE OF BENNINGTON
AUGUST 16 1777
A view of the action taken from the south-east: Baum's disposition is shown, as are the routes taken by
Stark's units during their attack, and the advance and repulse of Breymann's corps late in the day.

PHASE 2: 15.00

Having taken all morning to encircle Baum's forces, Herrick and Nichol drive off the Indians and commence their assaults on the main position: meanwhile Hobart and Stickney attack from the south-east, and Stark leads the reserve across the river flats against the enemy's eastern flank.

BRITISH (red) / **GERMAN** (light blue)
1 Fraser's Marksmen
2 Dragoons (three squadrons)
3 Indians
4 Grenadiers (detachment)
5 Light Infantry (detachment)
6 Peter's Loyalists
7 Canadians (in fortified cabins)
8 Baggage
9 Hesse Hanau artillery (two 3pdr guns)
10 Pfister's Loyalists
11 Grenadiers (main body)
12 Light Infantry (main body)
13 Hesse Hanau artillery (two 6pdr guns)

AMERICAN (dark blue)
A Nichol
B Hobart
C Stickney
D Herrick
E Reserve under Stark
F Reinforcement sent to Nichols
G Warner and Green Mountain Boys
H Vermont Rangers
J Prisoners

X
BAUM
(750)

WALLOOMSAC
RIVER

TO BENNINGTON

XX
STARK
(2,000)

N

PHASE 1: MORNING

Stark forms four columns under Herrick, Nichol, Hobart and Stickney. Nichol swings round to hit Baum's position from the north, as Hobart and Stickney approach the Loyalist and Canadian positions by the bridge; meanwhile Herrick circles to the south behind a wooded ridge, recrosses the river and attacks from the west.

Brigadier General Nicholas Herkimer (1728-77) at Oriskany, by F. Yohn.

The wounded Herkimer, propped up against his saddle under a beech tree, directs the battle. Noticing that his men were being 'rushed' by Indians while reloading, he told them to fight in pairs, with one man always being loaded. Ten days later, he died from a botched attempt to amputate his injured leg. Though a native-born American, he was a central figure in the Mohawk Valley's Palatine German community (preferring to speak German), and in July had tried unsuccessfully to negotiate Brant's neutrality. (Trustees of Utica Public Library)

By mid-morning on August 6, Herkimer had still heard nothing. His colonels demanded action, accusing him of cowardice and reminding him he had at least one relation in St Leger's force. Stung by their insubordination, and marginally reassured by the arrival of 60 Oneidas and 50 rangers, he gave the order to march. By 09.00, they had reached a point where the road was intersected by two steep-sided ravines, the first 700 feet wide and 50 feet deep, the second smaller, but deep enough to hide men from view. Both ravines were heavily shaded by trees, which grew within a few feet of the causeway. As Herkimer's leading regiment began to exit the second ravine, three whistles were heard.

Johnson had sited his ambush well. His own regiment blocked the road and lined the sides of the second ravine; the rest of the trail was flanked by Iroquois, under Brant, and the British rangers. They would allow the enemy van into the small ravine and the wagons and rearguard into the larger, then close the trap. The first part worked perfectly: the first volley wounded Herkimer and threw the head of the column into confusion. Unfortunately, the Iroquois attacked the rearguard too soon, pursuing them eastwards. This finished Visscher's regiment as a fighting unit, but also left an escape route, allowing the militia to fight their way back along the road in small groups and rally on higher ground.

Around 11.00, a thunderstorm halted the fighting for over an hour, giving Herkimer time to reorganize. Around noon, men wearing drab coats and odd hats, but marching in good order, appeared from the direction of the fort. Assuming they were Continentals, the militia allowed them to close; in fact, they were more 'Royal Greens', under Major Stephen Watts, wearing their coats inside-out. An alert militia officer spotted the ruse and persuaded his men to fire, whereupon desperate hand-to-hand fighting followed. As both sides withdrew to recover, three cannon shots were heard. Herkimer and his men knew instantly what they meant; and their enemies found out soon enough, as messengers arrived to tell Brant that his camp was being sacked. Already demoralized by heavy losses, the threat to their possessions persuaded the remaining warriors to leave, and with insufficient numbers to fight on unsupported, Johnson also withdrew.

Herkimer's messengers had arrived at the fort around 10.00 (St Leger's men saw them entering and realized their purpose) and after waiting for the thunder storm to pass, 250 men had attacked the Loyalist and Indian camps, removing 21 wagon-loads of supplies and materiel (most usefully the Indians' blankets and cooking utensils) without a casualty. The loss infuriated Brant's braves, who finished the day with nothing but their breech-cloths and weapons.

Herkimer reluctantly ordered a retreat to Fort Dayton. Barely 150 men from his three leading regiments were unhurt (Visscher's losses went unrecorded, but skeletons were found three miles away) and with insufficient fit men to carry the wounded, runners had to summon boats to collect the casualties. British losses were around 150.

The siege of Fort Stanwix
That night, Gansevoort received word from two officers captured at Oriskany, advising surrender. The following day, he met two British officers who stated that further resistance would leave St Leger powerless to control the Indians. Gansevoort refused to surrender, but agreed a three-day armistice, during which his second-in-command, Lieutenant Colonel Marinus Willett, took a message to Schuyler.

Despite Burgoyne's presence just 24 miles away, Schuyler decided he could afford to send a force to Fort Stanwix, and he ordered Arnold to march to Fort Dayton with 950 Continentals. Arriving on August 21, Arnold found only 100 militia willing to accompany him, but he pressed on, aware that St Leger's trenches were within 150 yards of the north-west bastion. To reduce the odds, Arnold ordered Hon Yost Schuyler[3] (who was awaiting trial as a Loyalist) to tell the Iroquois that 3,000 Continentals were coming, while he held Schuyler's brother hostage. Whether this story influenced the Indians is debatable, as they were already on the verge of abandoning St Leger. However, as they prepared to go, they became drunk, ransacked the British lines and forced St Leger to abandon the siege and his artillery. Arnold arrived on the evening of August 23: the next morning, a detachment sent to catch St Leger arrived at Lake Oneida just in time to see him sail away.

The raid on Bennington
Meanwhile, unaware of St Leger's failure, but only too aware (from a letter he kept concealed from his colleagues for several days) that Howe was not coming, Burgoyne had several problems to resolve. The Dragoons needed horses; the Loyalists needed recruits; and the army

Lieutenant Colonel Marinus Willett (1740-1830), by R Earl. **Willett had served briefly at Fort Stanwix during the French and Indian Wars, as well as at Fort Ticonderoga and Frontenac. A rabble-rousing Son of Liberty in New York City, he had joined the 1st New York Regiment in 1775 and fought in Canada, where he commanded the St John's garrison. He later served at New York City before being transferred to Fort Stanwix as Gansevoort's second-in-command, distinguishing himself in the sortie of August 6. He subsequently fought at Monmouth, then retired, but was persuaded to command militia levies during the Loyalist/Indian raids of 1781. (Metropolitan Museum of Art, New York)**

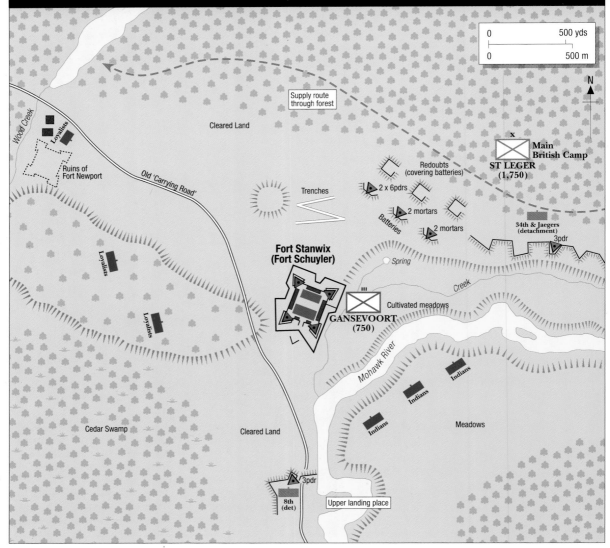

needed food and wagons. Burgoyne decided to send a large foraging expedition into New Hampshire to fulfil these needs and to disrupt the area from Manchester to Bennington, as far east as the Connecticut River. To lead this expedition, he chose Lieutenant Colonel Baum (who spoke no English), with Colonel Skene as liaison officer. However, while Burgoyne knew that Warner had retreated to Manchester, he did not know that the newly appointed Brigadier General John Stark had marched 1,492 New Hampshire militia to Bennington, or that Warner had been reinforced by 200 rangers.

After two weeks at Fort Edward, Burgoyne moved his army to Fort Miller. He also sent Simon Fraser's Advance Corps across the Hudson to harass Schuyler at Saratoga and prevent him sending troops after Baum. As Baum left Fort Miller on August 11 his orders were changed: new intelligence had suggested that Bennington was an important depot, guarded by just 300 militia, so this was now his first objective.

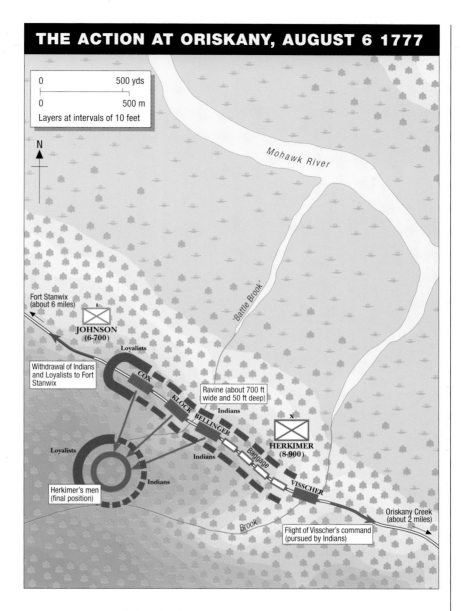

THE ACTION AT ORISKANY, AUGUST 6 1777

0 — 500 yds
0 — 500 m
Layers at intervals of 10 feet

N

Mohawk River

'Battle Brook'

Fort Stanwix
(about 6 miles)

JOHNSON
(6-700)

Loyalists

Withdrawal of Indians
and Loyalists to Fort
Stanwix

COX

KLOCK

BELLINGER

Ravine (about 700 ft
wide and 50 ft deep)

Indians

HERKIMER
(8-900)

Loyalists

Indians

Baggage

Herkimer's men
(final position)

Indians

VISSCHER

Oriskany Creek
(about 2 miles)

Brook

Flight of Visscher's command
(pursued by Indians)

Baum reached Cambridge in two days, during which time, however, his Indian contingent so terrorized the area that farmers hid their cattle (any the Indians did find were killed for their bells) and horses, and Loyalists stayed home to protect their families. Stark sent 200 militia to Sancoick's Mill to delay Baum (who informed Burgoyne that up to 1,800 militia were now reported at Bennington, which he planned to attack the next day) and late on August 14 Stark's main force faced Baum across the Walloomsac River. Stark fell back to await Warner, while Baum occupied a hill overlooking the bridge and sent for help. It rained all the next day; but 500 militia and Stockbridge Indians joined Stark, while Baum was reinforced by 150 Loyalists under a retired British officer called Pfister.

Baum posted his dragoons with one gun and half of Captain Fraser's Marksmen atop a 300-foot hill, behind a log breastwork (the ground being too stony for a proper earthwork). At the south-east base of the hill

Fort Stanwix (Schuyler): the north wall and ditch viewed from the north-west bastion. **This illustrates the role of the bastion – providing flanking fire against attacks on the curtain wall – and shows the palisaded 'covered way' on the glacis, and the 'fraise' on the wall above the ditch. St Leger's siege lines formed a triangle: 500 yards to the north-east (just beyond the buildings at left) lay the main batteries, guarded by his regulars; 800 yards to the south was the Lower Landing, held by some Loyalists and a few regulars; a third post, a half-mile away at Wood Creek, was also manned by Loyalists. A cordon of Indians linked these positions and a separate group guarded the opposite bank at the Lower Landing. (Author's photograph)**

was a picket of 50 jaegers; to the west, in a field, was the baggage park, guarded by 50 German grenadiers, Pfister's men, and the Indians. Lower down the hill, the remaining Marksmen and 50 German infantry with another 3pdr covered the bridge, either side of which were some cabins, held by the Canadians. Peters' corps occupied an earthwork covering a rise south-west of the bridge.

Stark and Warner (who had arrived ahead of his men) decided to risk dividing their forces in order to attack from all sides at once. Two columns would assault the bridge, supported by the reserve; two more would circle the hill and assault it from the north, the one with the longest distance to travel giving the signal to start the attack.[4]

At 12.00 on August 16, the rain having ceased, the columns moved off. Around 15.00, men were seen in the woods north of the main redoubt: based on Skene's opinion that Loyalists outnumbered rebels five to one in the area (small parties of 'Loyalists' had joined and left the column at will since Cambridge), Baum assumed they were friendly. As Herrick and Nichol closed in, there was heavy fighting around the redoubt: the militia gradually picked off the gunners and reduced the dragoons each time they stood up to fire a volley. Nevertheless, the dragoons held on until their ammunition ran out; then they drew their swords and tried to cut their way out, but once Baum fell, mortally wounded, morale collapsed and the survivors surrendered.

Meanwhile, on the other side of the river, the southern columns had rushed Peters' men, taking the defenders' first volley then overrunning them as they reloaded: at this, the Canadians and Indians promptly fled. The British and German contingents were then overwhelmed by Stark's reserve, which also captured the jaegers picket at the base of the hill.

As Stark's men began plundering Baum's camp, word arrived of more enemy troops near Sancoick's Mill. This was a relief column, led by

Breymann, which Burgoyne had dispatched at 08.00 the previous day. Heavy rain and poor roads had restricted him to just eight miles, and by 16.30 the following day, he had only covered eleven more and was still six miles from Baum when he received news of the fighting. A mile further on, Breymann spotted armed men (whom Skene insisted were Loyalists, until they shot Breymann's horse). This was the first of four small groups Stark had sent to delay Breymann while he gathered what he could of his reserve. As Stark formed up on a wooded hill, north of the road, he was joined by Warner's command, who poured round both of Breymann's flanks. With his ammunition almost gone, Breymann ordered a withdrawal, but the Americans pressed forward and, as night fell, the retreat soon became a rout. Both 6pdrs were abandoned (Breymann was wounded trying to save them), and a third of the Germans were killed or captured: only darkness saved the rest.[5]

Burgoyne had lost almost 15 per cent of his command, leaving under 5,000 effectives. He wrote to Germain justifying the expedition, blaming Breymann's slow marching (and Riedesel for selecting Breymann, though both commanders were in fact Burgoyne's choice), and dramatically altering his views on local sympathy. He briefly considered withdrawing to Fort Edward to await developments, but decided to press on, despite his remaining Indians leaving him. Now, for the first time, the Americans could attack his outposts, though the balance was partly restored by the arrival of two Mohawk bands, the first of which brought news of St Leger's withdrawal. A week later, several British 'additional companies' (plus 222 German recruits) arrived from Canada, and Burgoyne set to work inducting them into his British regiments, along with the remaining 120 of the 600 Loyalists who had joined him since he had left Canada.

Having retreated to Stillwater, Schuyler – who had done so much to delay Burgoyne and force him to send Baum foraging – had been replaced by Gates on August 14, by order of Congress (Washington having refused to relieve Schuyler). As Schuyler expressed pity for his successor, who would still command only 6,000 men including militia, the glory of Bennington and the boost to American morale all fell to Gates' advantage. Soon after his arrival on August 19, he was joined by Morgan's elite riflemen and on September 1 Arnold returned from Fort Stanwix with 1,200 Continentals, allowing Gates to send Lincoln into Vermont to threaten Burgoyne's left.

Private, Braunschweig Dragoner Regiment, by F. von Germann. **Many myths surround this unit, such as the infamous 12-pound boots and 10-pound swords (in reality, neither weighed much more than four), and their discomfiture at being dismounted. In fact, with its Prussian-based training, the unit was used to acting on foot and had even learned 'tree fighting' tactics while in Canada. On the march, their sabers and jacked-boots were carried in the regimental baggage wagons, and they wore either gaiters or the striped overalls adopted by most of the German contingent. (Miriam and Ira D. Wallach Division, New York Public Library)**

Footnotes

1 Re-named Fort Schuyler in 1776 (and referred to as such in contemporary documents), it is usually called Fort Stanwix to avoid confusion with another Fort Schuyler, built in the French and Indian Wars, which lay 15 miles south-east of Fort Stanwix. The famous flag hoisted on August 3, made from a soldier's shirt and a woman's petticoat, was almost certainly not the first Stars and Stripes flown in action, as it had blue, as well as red and white, stripes, and no stars were described in the canton.

2 1st (Canajoharie), 2nd (Palatine), 3rd (Mohawk), and 4th (Kingsland/German Flats) regiments, commanded respectively by colonels Ebenezer Cox, Jacob Klock, Frederick Fisher (Visscher), and Peter Bellinger.

3 Schuyler was widely regarded as a simpleton by local whites, but conversely – as was often the case – was respected by the Indians. He was no relation to the American commander.

4 Stark's alleged exhortation 'We'll beat them before night, or Molly Stark will be a widow!' is interesting as his wife's name was Elizabeth.

5 Stark's men are often depicted as inexperienced farmers, in contrast to Baum's and Breymann's regulars. In fact, New Hampshire and Vermont were major recruiting areas in the French and Indian Wars and many men were former rangers or Provincials. Probably only Fraser's Marksmen and the Indians matched them in combat experience.

The Brunswick Dragoons at Bennington, August 16 1777. **The climax of the engagement at Bennington was the storming of the main redoubt, commanded by Lieutenant Colonel Baum himself and held by 200 dragoons, 25 rangers, and a 3pdr gun of the Hesse-Hanau artillery. Convinced that the Indians were patrolling the woods and that the Americans massing in them were Loyalist recruits, Baum did not realize his error until Nichol and Herrick attacked around 1500hrs. They were soon** joined by other American units which had overcome the defenses at the bridge. Outnumbered, surrounded, and almost out of ammunition, the dragoons were forced to draw their sabers and cut their way out through the woods and meadows to the south-west. About 30 dragoons, including Baum, reached the river, but they were intercepted and Baum was mortally wounded; only seven dragoons arrived back to Burgoyne, leaving the regiment with a single troop – barely quarter strength.

THE FIRST BATTLE

By September 8, Gates had reoccupied Schuyler's former position at Stillwater, but seeing that his right rested on a flat plain alongside the Hudson, offering his better-trained foe an obvious advantage, he moved three miles north to Bemis Heights, whose 100-foot slopes stopped just 200 yards from the river. Inland, the heights reached 300 feet, forming an irregular, heavily wooded plateau crossed from east to west by ravines, with isolated farms linked by obscure tracks. The only route which could carry an army was the main road to Albany, 20 miles to the south, which ran beside the river.

Gates' position was an inverted 'U' with sides three-quarters of a mile long, shrouded in trees (except by the river) that would impede enemy scouts. His engineer, the Pole Tadeusz Kosciuszko, proposed to protect his right with two lines of earthworks across the low ground by the river, commanded by a flanking battery, with three others on the hillside above; the center was covered by a ravine north of the Neilson Farm; the left flank was 'refused' to utilize some hills to the south-west (higher ground a half-mile further west was left unoccupied due to lack of men and time). A floating bridge was built opposite Bemis' Tavern, and Neilson's barn became a fort, with a battery either side linked by a breastwork of felled trees (though this last was not completed until October). To defend this position, Gates had 5,600 Continentals and 1,500 New York and Connecticut militia, with more militia coming (though most were heading south to replace the Continentals sent to Gates from the Highlands). He also called in Lincoln – who brought 700 men, leaving Warner at Manchester and patrols around Fort Ann and Fort Edward – and Stark, effectively removing the threat to Burgoyne's flank which had been carefully created by Schuyler. Stark refused, saying his men had measles (in fact it was pique at Lincoln's report of Bennington), then sent 800 men, who arrived on September 12, six days before their enlistments expired. Stark, arriving three days later, made no attempt to persuade them to stay.

Meanwhile, the opposing armies moved closer. On September 12, Burgoyne crossed the Hudson and on September 15, was advancing along the river road, while Fraser's Advance Corps followed the high ground to the west. However, progress was slow – just three miles a day – as the Americans had blocked the road and destroyed the bridges. The next day (September 16) was spent advancing three more miles to Sword's house, where Burgoyne halted for 48 hours while the road was cleared. That same day, Arnold attempted to ambush him, but failed to find a suitable position, though he did capture some foragers and disrupt the men mending the road.

Of more concern were the militia who had been massing on the east bank of the Hudson since September 9 and who had moved around

Tadeusz Kosciuszko (1746-1817), by J. Rhys. **Trained at the artillery and engineering school at Mézières, France, Kosciuszko had found little opportunity in his native Poland and, having become interested in philosophy and the concept of liberty, decided to go to America. Having helped design the Delaware forts protecting Philadelphia, he was given a Continental commission as colonel of engineers in October 1776 and sent to join Gates at Fort Ticonderoga (where he was highly critical of Baldwin's abilities). Unable to prevent the inevitable there, his subsequent selection and fortification of Bemis Heights did as much as any other single act to secure the outcome of the campaign. He later designed the defenses at West Point and served in the south (including the siege of Fort Ninety-Six, where his errors contributed to the successful defense of the post). (Independence National Historical Park)**

Bemis Heights, looking east to the Hudson River. **One of three batteries covering the defenses guarding the road to Albany and the Hudson River (hidden behind by the trees in the distance, at the far end of the cultivated fields). (Author's photograph)**

Fort Neilson, looking north-east. **The view from just in front of the Neilson Farm building, showing the ravine that covered most of the front of the American defenses. (Author's photograph)**

either side of Lake George and launched a three-pronged attack against the British rear. One column under Colonel Benjamin Woodbridge having already cleared Skenesboro and Fort Ann, another, led by Colonel John Brown, attacked the portage at Fort Ticonderoga on September 18, capturing four companies (156 men) of the 53rd, 119 Canadians, 63 artificers, a brig, several gunboats, and over 200 bateaux, as well as releasing over 100 prisoners. A third column, under Colonel Samuel Johnson, summoned Fort Ticonderoga, but Powell refused to surrender. Johnson and Brown withdrew down Lake George to attack Diamond Island. The garrison (two companies of the 47th) were alert and held out, so the militia burned the captured ships and returned via Skenesboro.

Freeman's Farm – September 19

On September 19, Burgoyne learned that Morgan's riflemen were in an exposed position three miles away, with Gates' main force a half-mile to their rear. He divided his force into three. Riedesel, accompanied by Phillips, would march along the river road to 'pin' Gates' right, leaving the Hesse Hanau regiment and the 47th guarding the artillery park and baggage. Hamilton's brigade, with Jones' guns and Burgoyne and his staff, would follow the tracks towards Freeman's Farm. Fraser and Breymann, with 12 guns and led by the Indians and Loyalists, would

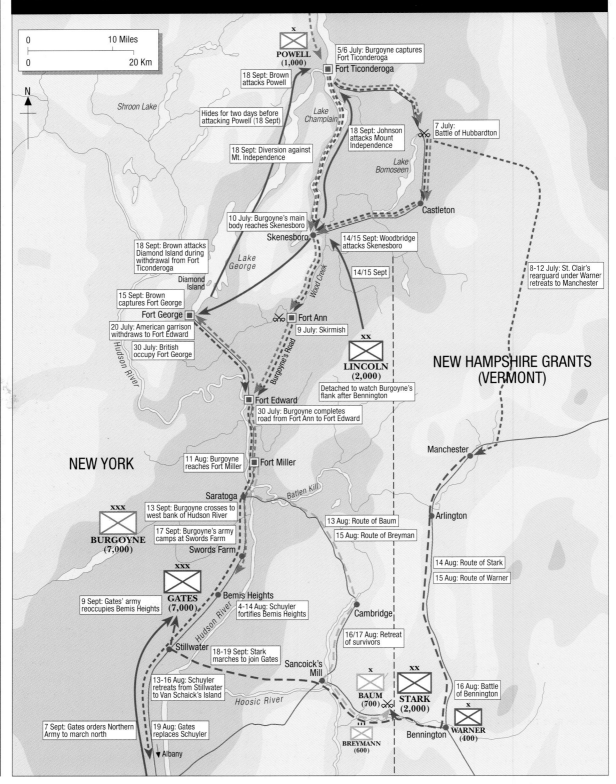

0   10 Miles

0   20 Km

N

POWELL
(1,000)

5/6 July: Burgoyne captures
Fort Ticonderoga

Fort Ticonderoga

18 Sept: Brown
attacks Powell

Shroon Lake

Hides for two days before
attacking Powell (18 Sept)

Lake
Champlain

7 July:
Battle of Hubbardton

18 Sept: Johnson
attacks Mount
Independence

18 Sept: Diversion against
Mt. Independence

Lake
Bomoseen

10 July: Burgoyne's main
body reaches Skenesboro

Castleton

Skenesboro

14/15 Sept: Woodbridge
attacks Skenesboro

18 Sept: Brown attacks
Diamond Island during
withdrawal from Fort
Ticonderoga

Lake
George

8-12 July: St. Clair's
rearguard under Warner
retreats to Manchester

Diamond
Island

14/15 Sept

Wood Creek

15 Sept: Brown
captures Fort George

Fort George

Fort Ann

9 July: Skirmish

20 July: American garrison
withdraws to Fort Edward

LINCOLN
(2,000)

**NEW HAMPSHIRE GRANTS
(VERMONT)**

30 July: British
occupy Fort George

Hudson River

Burgoyne's Road

Fort Edward

Detached to watch Burgoyne's
flank after Bennington

30 July: Burgoyne completes
road from Fort Ann to Fort Edward

NEW YORK

11 Aug: Burgoyne
reaches Fort Miller

Fort Miller

Manchester

Batten Kill

Saratoga

13 Sept: Burgoyne crosses to
west bank of Hudson River

13 Aug: Route of Baum

Arlington

BURGOYNE
(7,000)

17 Sept: Burgoyne's army
camps at Swords Farm

15 Aug: Route of Breyman

Swords Farm

14 Aug: Route of Stark

GATES
(7,000)

Bemis Heights

15 Aug: Route of Warner

9 Sept: Gates' army
reoccupies Bemis Heights

Hudson River

4-14 Aug: Schuyler
fortifies Bemis Heights

Cambridge

16/17 Aug: Retreat
of survivors

Stillwater

18-19 Sept: Stark
marches to join Gates

Sancoick's
Mill

16 Aug: Battle
of Bennington

13-16 Aug: Schuyler
retreats from Stillwater
to Van Schaick's Island

BAUM
(700)

STARK
(2,000)

Hoosic River

WARNER
(400)

7 Sept: Gates orders Northern
Army to march north

19 Aug: Gates
replaces Schuyler

BREYMANN
(600)

Bennington

Albany

Fort Neilson, looking north-west. **This shows the second battery and the reconstructed Neilson Farm (actually a small cabin, but typical of the 'farmhouses' dotted around the battlefield in 1777). The white stone marker at left is a memorial to Kosciuszko. (Author's photograph)**

Private, Regiment Prinz Friedrich, by F. von Germann. **The regiment garrisoned Fort Independence under Brigadier General Powell from mid-August until the withdrawal to Canada on November 8, and was thus the only Brunswick unit to escape intact, having survived, without loss, the attack on Fort Ticonderoga by American militia on September 18. (Miriam and Ira D. Wallach Division, New York Public Library)**

head west along a new road, then south towards Bemis Heights. Each column had a French-speaking liaison officer, and each would fire a signal gun when ready to attack. Despite suggestions that Burgoyne was aiming to envelop Gates' left, in reality he appears to have had no firm plan: however, he did have plenty of scouts, deserters, and local Tories to help his advance.

Around 9.00 the columns set off. About noon Hamilton crossed the Great Ravine unopposed, despite it being an excellent delaying spot, with steep, heavily wooded slopes and a substantial stream (even the small bridge was intact). He halted to allow the others to come abreast of him – Fraser had reached a ridge a half-mile west of Freeman's Farm, while Riedesel, delayed by blocked roads and broken bridges, had just sighted the river defenses. Three signal guns were fired and Hamilton resumed his advance, led by a 100-strong picket under Major Forbes (9th Foot).

Gates had received word from an officer on the east bank who had seen the British move off. Arnold immediately proposed an attack, but Gates decided to wait behind his defenses – in any event, he had no maps (nor, more culpably, had he patrolled the area). Disgusted by Gates' inaction, Arnold apparently sent Morgan forward, ordering Poor to support him. Morgan had barely arrived at Freeman's Farm when Forbes' picket emerged. The British were shot to pieces, losing every officer but one, and were then fired on by Hamilton's main body for good measure. Captain Fraser then led over some rangers, Indians, and Canadians to take Morgan in the flank, driving him back in disorder, but losing Captain Monin, which further demoralized the Canadians. It was 13.00.

After Jones had put a shot through the farmhouse to ensure it was empty, Hamilton moved forward and occupied a rise across the middle of the clearing, with the 20th so far back that the 62nd had to 'refuse' its two left companies. Jones placed two 6pdrs between the 9th and 21st and the other two between the two parts of the 62nd.

Meanwhile Fraser formed on Hamilton's right but separated by woods and streams, and around 14.00 the 1st New Hampshire contacted his outposts. The woods prevented either side judging the other's strength, but Cilley was forced back after 20 minutes. He rallied behind the 2nd and 3rd New Hampshire, who began firing into Hamilton's flank from the woods, forcing back the 9th, as Morgan's regrouped riflemen began picking off British officers and gunners.

Concerned, Fraser halted, sending five light companies to link with Hamilton and five companies of the 24th to clear Dearborn's men from a wood to his front. The latter were soon repulsed, but after Breymann's

Bemis Heights, looking west.
At the extreme left is the small hill that was incorporated into the defenses (the white dots in the ground denote the line of the earthworks). In the center (behind and to the left of the clump of trees) is the hill which was left unoccupied due to lack of time and manpower. The monument on the right was erected by the Daughters of the American Revolution to the Americans who fell at Saratoga. (Author's photograph)

grenadiers took their pursuers in the flank, the entire 24th attacked again and captured the wood, while more light companies outflanked Dearborn, and only the timely arrival of Lattimore saved him.

Gradually the fighting intensified: British bayonet charges were repulsed by heavy fire from opponents who, emerging from narrow tracks, could not form fast enough to counter-attack before being hit by artillery fire. The British began to see each appearance as fresh troops and Burgoyne, Hamilton, Fraser, and the newly arrived Phillips had to expose themselves to steady the line. British gunners were falling fast – 19 of the 22 crew of Hadden's 6pdrs were down – and the 62nd's left was becoming exposed. Two light companies plugged the gap temporarily, but with the guns silenced (and no sign of the four Phillips had ordered up) the Americans closed in. A bayonet charge by the 62nd was repulsed (one company had all 25 survivors captured) by an ad hoc force of 300 volunteers under Major William Hull (8th Massachusetts), commander of the pickets in front of Bemis Heights. Hull captured the guns, but found the tools had been removed and his men were driven back by the 20th, led by Phillips in person, while Burgoyne and Hamilton rallied the 62nd. On the right, Fraser, now facing the 2nd and 4th New York, had to commit Barner's battalion and the remaining British light infantry to hold his line.

Meanwhile Riedesel, hearing firing, had deployed his leading regiment (Specht) on the hills commanding the road, ordering them to build earthworks. After Phillips' departure, he had sent his adjutant to find Burgoyne and shifted westwards, sending patrols to locate Hamilton and scout the American lines in front. One patrol found a usable track: without awaiting orders, Riedesel left Specht to hold the road (with barely 1,000 men to guard the park and baggage as the 47th and Hesse Hanau regiments were well to the rear and did not arrive until 23.00) and led his own regiment, preceded by two companies of Rhetz and two 6pdrs, on the mile-long march uphill, through heavy woods.

Despite a deep, muddy ravine full of undergrowth and felled trees, Riedesel arrived in the nick of time. The two companies of Rhetz (led by their band and singing hymns) took Poor's right almost in the rear and forced it back into the woods south of Freeman's Farm. Pausch, running

a gauntlet of heavy fire as he passed behind the 20th and 62nd, arrived as the 9th and 21st were being forced off the rise, and quickly fired off a dozen rounds of canister as the Americans closed to within pistol range. When Riedesel's own regiment arrived and added its fire to that of the surviving British, the enemy withdrew, at which Pausch advanced, firing another dozen rounds into the woods as darkness fell.

On the right, Learned's brigade, which Arnold had finally got forward – either to cover Poor's withdrawal or to outflank Fraser – approached Fraser around 17.30, but was attacked by the British grenadiers and withdrew, leaving the 8th Massachusetts as a rearguard. Jaegers outflanked the 2nd New York, forcing it into a sunken path, where it held out until dark, and then drifted away.

By 18.30, the battle was over. The Americans had withdrawn in reasonable order, having inflicted heavier casualties on a slightly numerically superior enemy with artillery support (no American guns came into action). Although Arnold criticized his regimental commanders for performing junior roles instead of their own, no British bayonet charge had succeeded and but for Riedesel's intervention the British center would have collapsed. Given the 9th's losses at Fort Ann in July, with the 62nd down to 70 unwounded officers and men, the 20th and 21st in similar shape, and only 12 of Jones' 48 gunners unhurt, Hamilton's brigade was all but destroyed. Yet, at the same time, the Americans had missed the chance to capture Burgoyne's artillery park and baggage.

Next morning, warned by a deserter, the Americans stood to in the cold, dense fog. Arnold's men were still without ammunition after the previous day, and the army as a whole was down to 40 rounds each. Burgoyne, his wounded still coming in and his men eating their first meal in 24 hours, refused his right flank and camped as near the enemy as the terrain allowed, while his scouts probed Gates' lines. Riedesel and Hamilton remained where they had ended the battle, occupying a two-mile front from the Hudson to Freeman's Farm (now defended by a large redoubt), each regiment having a guard post to its front. North-west of the farm, the Canadians fortified two cabins, while to their rear another redoubt was constructed. Burgoyne's engineer, Lieutenant

Colonel Daniel Morgan (1736-1802), by C.W. Peale. **Morgan (here depicted as a general) commanded the only rifle-armed unit in Gates' army, and he and his men played a decisive role in the campaign. A veteran of the French and Indian Wars (in which he lost half his teeth to an Indian musket ball and was flogged for striking a British officer) and Pontiac's Rebellion, the 'old Waggoner' raised a rifle company in Virginia at the outbreak of war, serving under Arnold in Canada. Captured at Quebec and exchanged in 1776, he was commissioned colonel of the 11th Virginia and spent the early part of 1777 with Washington in New Jersey, before heading north in August. (Independence National Historical Park)**

Burgoyne's army reaches Sword's House (September 17) and establishes camp. Learning that strong American defenses overlook the Hudson River, and with no road capable of carrying his entire army, he plans a three-pronged advance to outflank Gates to the west and overrun his positions on Bemis Heights.

HUDSON RIVER

TAYLOR FARM

22

15

GREAT RAVIN

21

16

18

17

22

19

20

8

14

23

SWORD'S HOUSE

13

12

11

15

10

9

11

5

6

4

NORTH RAVINE

7

1

3

2

XX

RIEDESEL (2,000)

X

HAMILTON (1,500)

XXX

BURGOYNE (7,500)

X

FRASER (2,000)

PHASE 2: 11.00 TO 12.30, SEPTEMBER 19

After a delay to allow the fog to clear, Burgoyne's three columns advance towards the American lines: the right and center make good progress but Riedesel has to stop frequently to repair bridges. Despite regular reports from the east bank of the Hudson, Arnold has to force Gates to send Morgan and Dearborn forward.

FIRST BATTLE OF SARATOGA (FREEMAN'S FARM) – THE OPENING MOVES, SEPTEMBER 17–19 1777

A view taken from the north-west showing the initial deployments prior to the clash at Freeman's Farm: Burgoyne's camp around Sword's House (September 17–19) is shown, along with the routes of his three columns on September 19 up to the firing of the first shots.

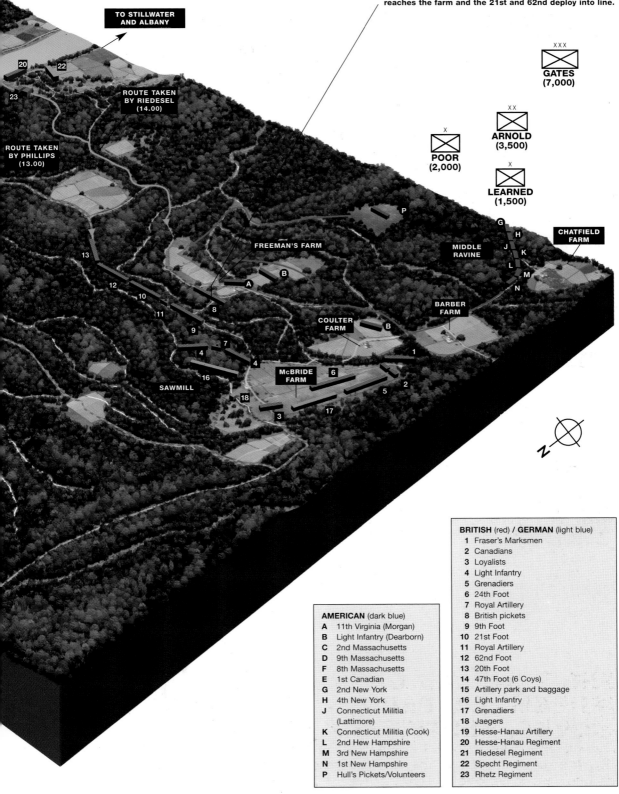

Hamilton's pickets at Freeman's Farm are surprised and driven back by Morgan's riflemen, whose follow-up charge is then repulsed. Morgan rallies his men and Dearborn extends the American line westwards as Hamilton's main body reaches the farm and the 21st and 62nd deploy into line.

TO STILLWATER AND ALBANY

ROUTE TAKEN BY RIEDESEL (14.00)

ROUTE TAKEN BY PHILLIPS (13.00)

GATES (7,000)

POOR (2,000)

ARNOLD (3,500)

LEARNED (1,500)

FREEMAN'S FARM

MIDDLE RAVINE

CHATFIELD FARM

COULTER FARM

BARBER FARM

McBRIDE FARM

SAWMILL

N

AMERICAN (dark blue)
A   11th Virginia (Morgan)
B   Light Infantry (Dearborn)
C   2nd Massachusetts
D   9th Massachusetts
F   8th Massachusetts
E   1st Canadian
G   2nd New York
H   4th New York
J   Connecticut Militia
      (Lattimore)
K   Connecticut Militia (Cook)
L   2nd Hew Hampshire
M   3rd New Hampshire
N   1st New Hampshire
P   Hull's Pickets/Volunteers

BRITISH (red) / **GERMAN** (light blue)
1   Fraser's Marksmen
2   Canadians
3   Loyalists
4   Light Infantry
5   Grenadiers
6   24th Foot
7   Royal Artillery
8   British pickets
9   9th Foot
10   21st Foot
11   Royal Artillery
12   62nd Foot
13   20th Foot
14   47th Foot (6 Coys)
15   Artillery park and baggage
16   Light Infantry
17   Grenadiers
18   Jaegers
19   Hesse-Hanau Artillery
20   Hesse-Hanau Regiment
21   Riedesel Regiment
22   Specht Regiment
23   Rhetz Regiment

Lieutenant Colonel Henry Dearborn (1751-1829), by C.W. Peale.

A former medical student, Dearborn had been a militia officer when war broke out and having marched his men to Boston, distinguished himself under Stark's command at Bunker's Hill. He also served under Arnold in Canada. He was captured in the attack on Quebec City, but unlike Morgan, was not exchanged until March 1777. Promoted to major in the 3rd New Hampshire regiment, he was tasked with raising a light infantry corps from the Northern Army to serve alongside Morgan. So well did his unit perform up to and including September 19, that Dearborn was promoted to lieutenant colonel. (Independence National Historical Park)

Twiss, sited batteries at regular intervals and had trees felled up to 400 yards before each post. By the river, the 47th and the remaining Loyalists and Dragoons guarded the park, baggage, bateaux, hospital, and pontoon bridge, while the Hesse-Hanau regiment occupied the heights.

The Americans also extended their lines, using the militia and Con-tinental recruits who arrived daily. The two armies could hear each other, but (except by the river) could see only trees. As scouting, taking prisoners, and intercepting messages became vital, the arrival of 150 Oneida, Tuscarora, and Onondaga braves, and the simultaneous departure of Burgoyne's few remaining Ottawas, gave Gates an unbeatable advantage, while a constant stream of undernourished and disillusioned deserters provided the Americans with valuable intelligence on the state of Burgoyne's force.

Gates' only problem was Arnold. The animosity between them may

Looking north towards Freeman's Farm. **This was the view Morgan's men had around midday on September 19, as they ambushed Forbes' pickets. The farm's owner, John Freeman, had fled to Canada and returned with Burgoyne's army: in September 1777, the land was being farmed by Isaac Leggett, a Loyalist Quaker. (Author's photograph)**

have become exaggerated with time – it certainly figures little in contemporary writing – but Gates did try to limit Arnold's influence on events, perhaps understandably, given Arnold's propensity for inviting battle with a superior enemy. Gates put Morgan and Dearborn under his own direct command and assigned three New York militia regiments to Glover, instead of Poor. However, the final straw was his message of September 26, congratulating the army for the action at Freeman's Farm, without mentioning anyone from Arnold's division. When Arnold protested at the 'slight', Gates relieved him of command and dismissed him from the camp, giving Lincoln the right wing and himself the left. Whether from peer pressure or bloody-mindedness, Arnold did not go.

Meanwhile, one message did reach Burgoyne: on September 21, he learned that Clinton was moving up the Hudson and would attack Fort Montgomery the next day.[1]

BELOW *Looking south from Freeman's Farm.* **The 15-acre farm formed an oblong that ran east-west, crossing the vertical arm of the T-shaped ridge on which the farm and other buildings stood. (Author's photograph)**

THE ROYAL ARTILLERY AT FREEMAN'S FARM, SEPTEMBER 19 1777. The fate of the Royal Artillery detachment under Second Lieutenant James Hadden at Freeman's Farm illustrates the heavy losses inflicted on British officers and gun crews by American marksmen throughout the campaign. Hadden's two light 6pdrs covered the angle formed by the refusal of the two left companies of the 62nd Foot, which was being attacked from front, flank, and rear.

By about 16.00, only Hadden and three of his 22 men were not killed or wounded: after requesting help to fight his guns, during which a bullet went through the front of his cap, Hadden was joined by the senior artillery officer with Hamilton's brigade, Captain Thomas Jones. Within minutes Jones and the 11 men with him had also fallen, Hadden himself carrying Jones to safety as the enemy finally overran the guns.

Clinton in the Hudson Highlands

Clinton had under 7,000 men – including 3,000 untrained Loyalists – to defend the 100 miles from Long Island, via Manhattan, to Paulus Hook and New Jersey, although another 1,700 regulars (mainly seasick recruits) arrived in September. He had no orders to assist Burgoyne, and though free to exercise his own judgement, could only act on Burgoyne's last message (dated August 6) saying Burgoyne would reach Albany by August 23! Rumors about Bennington merely suggested to him that Burgoyne had feinted eastwards, and the first indication Clinton had that all was not well was Burgoyne's reply of September 21.[2]

The American Hudson Highland defenses were weak. Putnam, with 1,200 Continentals and some militia, held the east bank around Peekskill and Fort Independence. On the other side, north of Bear Mountain, stood Fort Clinton and Fort Montgomery, a half-mile apart and either side of a deep ravine called Popolopen Kill. Commanded by the Clinton brothers, George and James, Fort Clinton was the smaller, but almost finished: Fort Montgomery was the larger, but incomplete. Together they mounted 67 guns, but their garrisons (5th New York and one company of 2nd Continental Artillery – 500 men) were inadequate. However, the terrain favored defense: the river, 100 feet below, was narrow and swift, blocked by a log boom and chain, and guarded by two

Brigadier General James Clinton (1733-1812), by J. Sharples. **Clinton served in Canada and was made brigadier general in August 1776. He commanded Fort Montgomery, from which he escaped, despite a bayonet wound. (Independence National Historical Park)**

24-gun frigates (*Congress* and *Montgomery*), an armed sloop, and two row galleys (none fully equipped or manned). Further north, Fort Constitution, opposite West Point, was still under construction, and there were clusters of *chevaux-de-frise* lining the river-bed.

On October 3 Clinton started up the Hudson with 3,000 men, three frigates, and various smaller vessels. Warned by spies, Putnam assumed it was a foraging raid and did not call out the militia or speed up work on his defenses. Two days later, Clinton landed at Verplank's Point, suggesting an attack on Peekskill that forced Putnam into the hills, abandoning Fort Independence, and imploring the west bank garrisons to join him. Meanwhile, George Clinton had ordered out the militia, but barely 300 reached the forts since it was harvest time.

Clinton now received another message from Burgoyne: down to 5,000 men, Burgoyne faced 10,000 Americans, with more in his rear. Although confident he could still reach Albany, his men would need feeding – could Clinton reach Albany and supply him from New York City? He also asked Clinton for orders to advance or retreat before the lakes froze, adding that he had only left Fort Edward because he expected a relief force to meet him at Albany.

On October 6, Clinton landed at Stony Point, divided his 2,000 men into two groups, and stormed both forts. The Americans lost 250 of 600

ABOVE *Looking west from Freeman's Farm.* **This was where the 21st Foot fought on September 19, with the 9th to its right – beyond the trees – linking with Fraser's Advance Corps. (Author's photograph)**

BELOW *Looking east from Freeman's Farm.* **This was probably the 'slight rise' occupied by Hadden's guns and the two 'refused' companies of the 62nd Foot on September 19, with the American attacks coming mainly from the trees on the right of the picture. Pausch's guns would have followed the tree-line on the left as they passed behind the British infantry, while the faint line 'snaking' across the open space in the left-center is roughly the route of Riedesel's advance against the American right rear. (Author's photograph)**

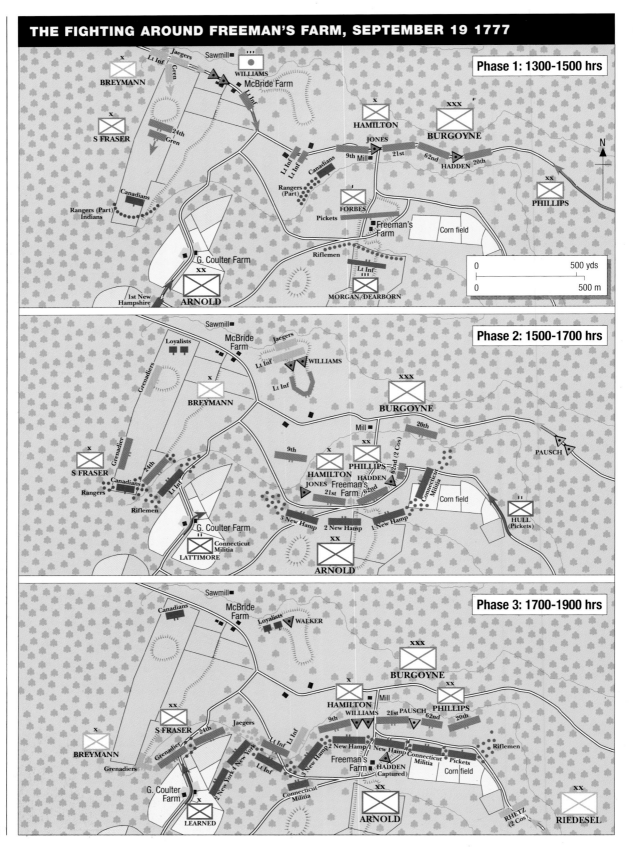

THE FIGHTING AROUND FREEMAN'S FARM, SEPTEMBER 19 1777

Phase 1: 1300-1500 hrs

BREYMANN
Jaegers
Lt Inf
Gren
Sawmill
WILLIAMS
McBride Farm
Lt Inf
S FRASER
24th
Gren
HAMILTON
BURGOYNE
JONES
9th
Mill
21st
62nd
HADDEN
20th
Lt Inf
Lt Inf
Canadians
Rangers (Part)
Canadians
PHILLIPS
Rangers (Part) Indians
FORBES
Pickets
Freeman's Farm
Corn field
N
G. Coulter Farm
ARNOLD
Riflemen
Lt Inf
0   500 yds
0   500 m
1st New Hampshire
MORGAN/DEARBORN

Phase 2: 1500-1700 hrs

Sawmill
McBride Farm
Loyalists
Jaegers
Lt Inf
WILLIAMS
Lt Inf
BREYMANN
Grenadiers
BURGOYNE
Mill
20th
Grenadier
9th
62nd (2 Cos)
PAUSCH
S FRASER
24th
HAMILTON
PHILLIPS
Canadians
Lt Inf
JONES
HADDEN
Rangers
Freeman's
Farm
21st
62nd
Riflemen
Connecticut Militia
Corn field
G. Coulter Farm
3 New Hamp
2 New Hamp
1 New Hamp
HULL (Pickets)
Connecticut Militia
LATTIMORE
ARNOLD

Phase 3: 1700-1900 hrs

Sawmill
Canadians
McBride Farm
Loyalists
WALKER
BURGOYNE
S FRASER
24th
Jaegers
Lt Inf
Lt Inf
HAMILTON
Mill
9th
WILLIAMS
21st
PAUSCH
62nd
20th
PHILLIPS
BREYMANN
Grenadier
Grenadiers
Lt Inf
2 New Hamp
New Hamp
Riflemen
2 New York
4 New York
3 New Hamp
Freeman's
Farm
Connecticut Militia
Pickets
Corn field
G. Coulter Farm
Lt Inf
Connecticut Militia
HADDEN (Captured)
LEARNED
ARNOLD
RHETZ (2 Cos)
RIEDESEL

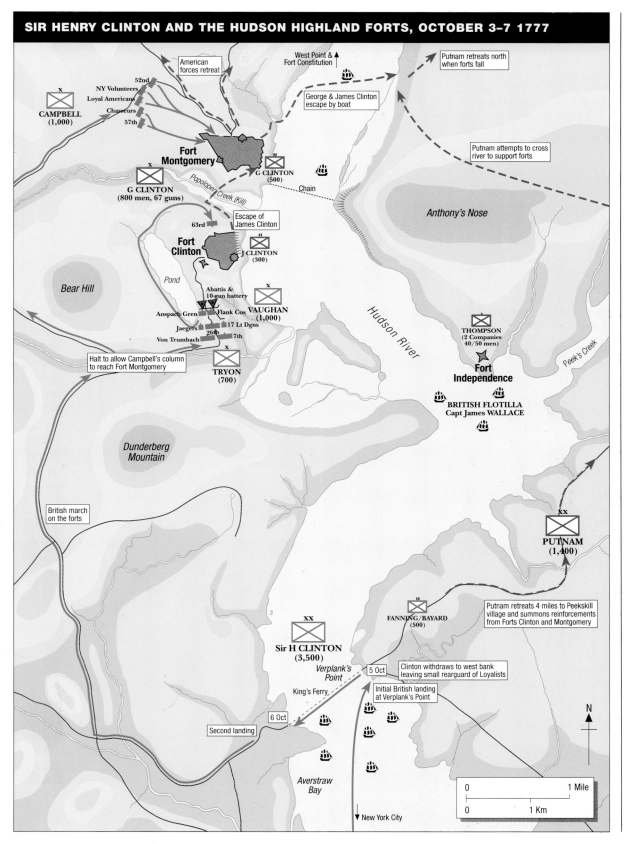

American forces retreat

52nd

NY Volunteers
Loyal Americans
Chasseurs
57th

CAMPBELL
(1,000)

West Point &
Fort Constitution

Putnam retreats north
when forts fall

George & James Clinton
escape by boat

Putnam attempts to cross
river to support forts

Fort Montgomery

G CLINTON
(500)

Chain

Popolopen Creek (Kill)

G CLINTON
(800 men, 67 guns)

Anthony's Nose

63rd

Escape of
James Clinton

Fort Clinton

J CLINTON
(300)

Bear Hill

Pond

Abattis &
10-gun battery

Anspach Gren   Flank Cos

Jaegers   17 Lt Dgns

Von Trumbach   26th   7th

VAUGHAN
(1,000)

Hudson River

THOMPSON
(2 Companies
40/50 men)

Peek's Creek

Fort Independence

Halt to allow Campbell's column
to reach Fort Montgomery

TRYON
(700)

BRITISH FLOTILLA
Capt James WALLACE

Dunderberg Mountain

British march
on the forts

PUTNAM
(1,400)

Putnam retreats 4 miles to Peekskill
village and summons reinforcements
from Forts Clinton and Montgomery

FANNING/BAYARD
(500)

Sir H CLINTON
(3,500)

Verplank's Point

5 Oct

Clinton withdraws to west bank
leaving small rearguard of Loyalists

King's Ferry

Initial British landing
at Verplank's Point

6 Oct

Second landing

Averstraw Bay

↓ New York City

N
↑

0   1 Mile
0   1 Km

Brigadier General George Clinton (1739-1812) by J. Sharples.

A radical lawyer who had challenged Schuyler as leader of the revolutionary minority in the New York assembly, George Clinton was cut out for politics rather than active service, and he had no illusions about his limitations. Appointed a general in the Continental Line in 1777, he was also New York's first state governor, and was responsible for organizing its defenses. Despite losing the Hudson forts and failing to protect Esopus, he won a reputation as an effective wartime governor, serving six consecutive terms and opposing Loyalist and Indian raids from Canada throughout 1779 and 1780. The Clinton brothers were unrelated to Sir Henry Clinton, the British general. (Art Commission of the City of New York)

(the rest escaping into the woods) and the British 40 dead and 150 wounded. At the same time, the flotilla under Sir James Wallace broke the boom and burned or captured every American vessel before heading up-river to summon Fort Constitution, whose garrison fled as Clinton arrived. Establishing a base at Fort Clinton (which dominated Fort Montgomery) Clinton summoned more troops, six months' supplies, and more transports, but had to return to New York City as the two ranking British generals there were ill (leaving a Hessian officer of dubious merits in overall command). Further progress was entrusted to Major General John Vaughan.

Footnotes

1 American losses were 100 dead, 325 wounded, and 40 missing: officially, the British lost 160 dead, 364 wounded, and 42 missing, but this may exclude Loyalists, Canadians, and Indians – one British report mentions over 500 wounded.

2 Burgoyne's reply – agreeing to Clinton's plan – was delivered to Clinton on September 29 by Captain Campbell (62nd Foot), who returned with another missive from Clinton explaining that he had done what he had promised but was in no position to give Burgoyne orders. This reached Burgoyne on October 16, just hours after the Convention was signed. A message that the forts had fallen was carried by Lieutenant Taylor (9th Foot), who was unluckily caught by men of Webb's Additional Continental Regiment (who wore red coats): despite twice swallowing the message (in a silver bullet), Taylor was discovered and hanged as a spy on October 18.

THE SECOND BATTLE

October 3 brought Burgoyne's army news of Howe's victory at Brandywine but also a cut in rations, while deserters provided Gates with a constant flow of information and his scouts attacked outposts and intercepted messages. The militia cut communications with Fort Ticonderoga, destroyed bridges, and halted foraging on the still-fertile west bank of the Hudson. Burgoyne called frequent councils of war, increasingly rationalizing his inaction as preventing Gates from joining Washington. One such council discussed a proposal to leave 800 men in camp and storm Gates' left flank and rear under an artillery bombardment. Riedesel advised a tactical withdrawal to Batten Kill to await news from Clinton and restore links with Fort Ticonderoga. Fraser and Hamilton agreed, but Burgoyne would not countenance a retreat. Instead, he spread rumors that Clinton was near: on the night of October 6, a signal rocket was fired, but if anyone was fooled, it was not for long – the Germans, especially, began comparing him unfavorably with Carleton.

On October 5 Burgoyne proposed a combined reconnaissance in force and foraging expedition, and if a general advance seemed feasible, the whole army would attack the next day: if not, it would retire to Batten Kill on October 11 (no reasons were given for the three-day delay). Captain Fraser's Marksmen, the Indians and the Loyalists would approach Gates' left rear by secret paths, while the main force – 2,000 picked men and ten guns – would head south from the Balcarres Redoubt at Freeman's Farm.

Bemis Heights – October 7

Another council of war, a meeting with the Indians, and a heavy mist all served to delay the start until 10.00. With frequent halts to flush out American pickets and make tracks passable for the guns, it took 30 minutes to reach a clearing barely 800 yards from the Balcarres Redoubt. The light infantry, 24th, and two guns occupied a low hill on the right, their right flank sharply refused and their left separated from the rest of the force by thick woods. Riedesel's 300-man detachment (drawn from all his four regiments) occupied a clearing: two 12pdrs guarded their front and Pausch's two 6pdrs their left. Acland's grenadiers formed a right angle to Riedesel, while the British line infantry (also made up of detachments) were parallel with Riedesel and extended the line to the knoll near the Balcarres Redoubt: the British units had four 6pdrs and two 5.5-inch and two 8-inch howitzers. Skirmishers covered the entire front and flanks, but the line was thin – barely a man per yard – and there were huge gaps. Behind them, Gall held the river, Hamilton and Specht the main camp, Major Campbell the Advance Corps positions, and Breymann the right. While foragers collected grain, staff officers climbed onto cabin roofs to observe Gates' lines. Inevitably, trees blocked their view.

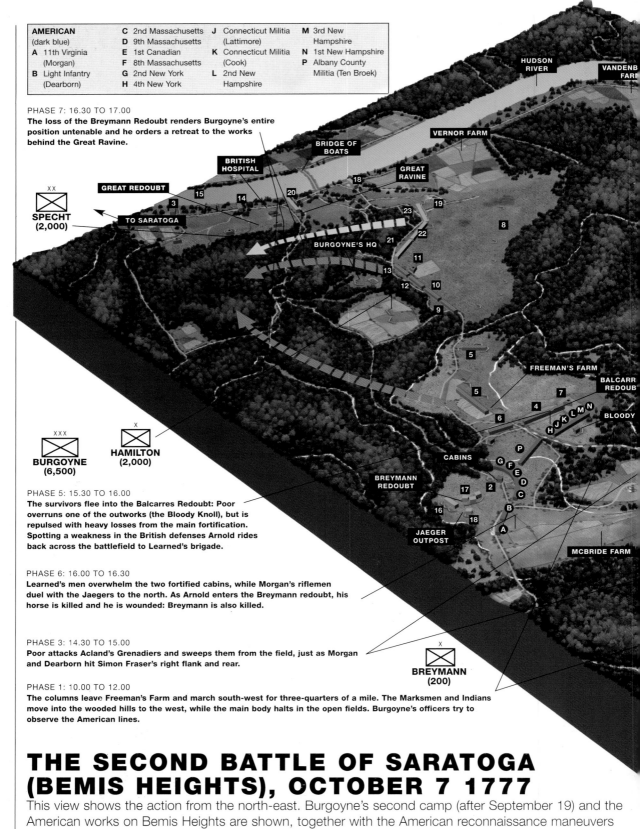

AMERICAN
(dark blue)
A 11th Virginia
  (Morgan)
B Light Infantry
  (Dearborn)
C 2nd Massachusetts
D 9th Massachusetts
E 1st Canadian
F 8th Massachusetts
G 2nd New York
H 4th New York
J Connecticut Militia
  (Lattimore)
K Connecticut Militia
  (Cook)
L 2nd New
  Hampshire
M 3rd New
  Hampshire
N 1st New Hampshire
P Albany County
  Militia (Ten Broek)

HUDSON RIVER

VANDENB FARM

PHASE 7: 16.30 TO 17.00
The loss of the Breymann Redoubt renders Burgoyne's entire position untenable and he orders a retreat to the works behind the Great Ravine.

VERNOR FARM

BRIDGE OF BOATS

BRITISH HOSPITAL

GREAT REDOUBT

GREAT RAVINE

XX
**SPECHT
(2,000)**

TO SARATOGA

BURGOYNE'S HQ

FREEMAN'S FARM

BALCARR REDOUB

BLOODY

XXX
**BURGOYNE
(6,500)**

X
**HAMILTON
(2,000)**

CABINS

PHASE 5: 15.30 TO 16.00
The survivors flee into the Balcarres Redoubt: Poor overruns one of the outworks (the Bloody Knoll), but is repulsed with heavy losses from the main fortification. Spotting a weakness in the British defenses Arnold rides back across the battlefield to Learned's brigade.

BREYMANN REDOUBT

JAEGER OUTPOST

MCBRIDE FARM

PHASE 6: 16.00 TO 16.30
Learned's men overwhelm the two fortified cabins, while Morgan's riflemen duel with the Jaegers to the north. As Arnold enters the Breymann redoubt, his horse is killed and he is wounded: Breymann is also killed.

PHASE 3: 14.30 TO 15.00
Poor attacks Acland's Grenadiers and sweeps them from the field, just as Morgan and Dearborn hit Simon Fraser's right flank and rear.

X
**BREYMANN
(200)**

PHASE 1: 10.00 TO 12.00
The columns leave Freeman's Farm and march south-west for three-quarters of a mile. The Marksmen and Indians move into the wooded hills to the west, while the main body halts in the open fields. Burgoyne's officers try to observe the American lines.

THE SECOND BATTLE OF SARATOGA (BEMIS HEIGHTS), OCTOBER 7 1777

This view shows the action from the north-east. Burgoyne's second camp (after September 19) and the American works on Bemis Heights are shown, together with the American reconnaissance maneuvers and counter-attack.

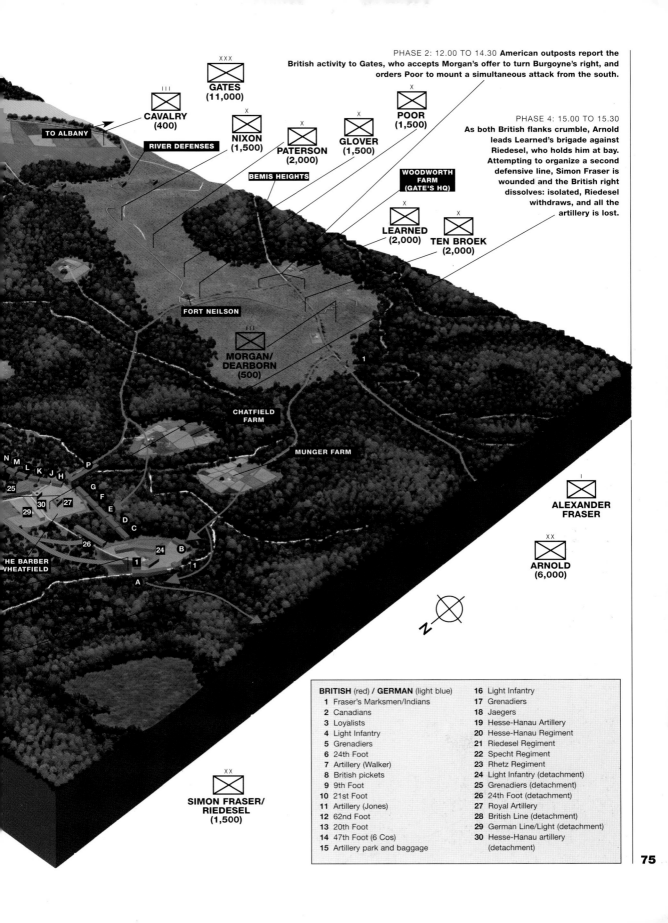

PHASE 2: 12.00 TO 14.30 **American outposts report the British activity to Gates, who accepts Morgan's offer to turn Burgoyne's right, and orders Poor to mount a simultaneous attack from the south.**

PHASE 4: 15.00 TO 15.30
As both British flanks crumble, Arnold leads Learned's brigade against Riedesel, who holds him at bay. Attempting to organize a second defensive line, Simon Fraser is wounded and the British right dissolves: isolated, Riedesel withdraws, and all the artillery is lost.

GATES
(11,000)

CAVALRY
(400)

TO ALBANY

RIVER DEFENSES

NIXON
(1,500)

PATERSON
(2,000)

BEMIS HEIGHTS

GLOVER
(1,500)

POOR
(1,500)

WOODWORTH
FARM
(GATE'S HQ)

LEARNED
(2,000)

TEN BROEK
(2,000)

FORT NEILSON

MORGAN/
DEARBORN
(500)

CHATFIELD
FARM

MUNGER FARM

ALEXANDER
FRASER

ARNOLD
(6,000)

N M L K J H
P
G
F
E
D
C
B
A
25
30
29
27
26
24
1
1

HE BARBER
WHEATFIELD

N

SIMON FRASER/
RIEDESEL
(1,500)

BRITISH (red) / **GERMAN** (light blue)	
1 Fraser's Marksmen/Indians	16 Light Infantry
2 Canadians	17 Grenadiers
3 Loyalists	18 Jaegers
4 Light Infantry	19 Hesse-Hanau Artillery
5 Grenadiers	20 Hesse-Hanau Regiment
6 24th Foot	21 Riedesel Regiment
7 Artillery (Walker)	22 Specht Regiment
8 British pickets	23 Rhetz Regiment
9 9th Foot	24 Light Infantry (detachment)
10 21st Foot	25 Grenadiers (detachment)
11 Artillery (Jones)	26 24th Foot (detachment)
12 62nd Foot	27 Royal Artillery
13 20th Foot	28 British Line (detachment)
14 47th Foot (6 Cos)	29 German Line/Light (detachment)
15 Artillery park and baggage	30 Hesse-Hanau artillery (detachment)

75

ABOVE *The Barber Wheatfield, looking west along the British line.* **The path on the right roughly follows the British line on October 7, with the viewer at the junction of the British Line contingent and Acland's Grenadiers. Riedesel was in the middle distance, with the 24th Foot beyond them: the light infantry were in another field, beyond the tree-line in the far distance. The white marker at the extreme right is where Fraser was shot while trying to form a rearguard. (Author's photograph)**

Gates now had over 11,000 men (more than half Continentals). He and his staff assumed that such a labored advance must be a feint and that Burgoyne's main effort would be against their right. Nevertheless, Gates sent two officers to reconnoiter and ordered Morgan forward, supported by Poor, Learned, and a small artillery detachment.

Around 15.00 Burgoyne saw small enemy groups drive in his outposts, then Poor's brigade emerge from the woods. Acland ordered his grenadiers to give a volley then charge, but they fired too high and Poor's men slaughtered them,[1] captured their guns, and cut off most of Burgoyne's force from their line of retreat. Learned now emerged opposite the Germans, concealed in the crops. Riedesel's men rose and fired, but Learned drove them back, capturing the two 12pdrs and their commander, Major Williams. Pausch, now isolated, withdrew to where Riedesel's men had rallied, took post in an abandoned earthwork, and repulsed two fierce assaults.

Meanwhile, Morgan had circled around Simon Fraser's right rear and, as the light infantry turned to face him, Dearborn drove them off the hill

with a volley and bayonet charge. Balcarres rallied his men behind a fence, but Morgan again appeared behind them as Dearborn attacked their front. With the 24th away replacing Acland's grenadiers, the light infantry lacked support and were forced back, exposing Riedesel's rear.

Crowds of foragers and casualties now filled the road, and with the artillery horses being picked off, Burgoyne saw disaster looming. He sent his aide, Sir Francis Clarke, to order Phillips and Riedesel to withdraw, while he rode back to organize the defense of the camp, but Clarke was mortally wounded before he could reach them. As Ten Broeck's brigade arrived to support Learned, Pausch tried to remove his guns, but he was overrun and could only escape with an ammunition wagon as his gunners fled into the woods.

Fraser, forming a rearguard of the 24th and the light infantry, held the Americans at bay, until – on orders from Arnold and Morgan – a rifleman shot him in the stomach. As he was carried to the rear, Balcarres took over and withdrew to his redoubt. It had taken less than a hour to rout Burgoyne's entire force and capture its ten guns. However, the fighting was

BELOW *The Barber Wheatfield, looking north.* **As they emerged from the woods, Poor and Learned attacked roughly to the right and left (respectively) of the two bushes in the center, while Ten Broeck's brigade arrived from the extreme right. The stone circle and gun in the previous shot are on the slight rise at the far right, beside the tall tree. (Author's photograph)**

far from over. Poor's brigade now chased Balcarres, storming the outwork (later christened the 'Bloody Knoll') and led by Arnold (variously described by those who saw him as 'mad', 'drunk', and 'suicidally courageous') attacked the Balcarres Redoubt itself. Repulsed with considerable losses, Poor withdrew, but kept the fort under heavy fire.

Behind Poor, Learned and Morgan swung east, attacking the cabins and the Breymann Redoubt, the latter manned by barely 200 men. Breymann withstood one rush, but the Americans found dead ground, and with the jaegers on the knoll pinned down by heavy fire, Morgan

BENEDICT ARNOLD AT THE BREYMANN REDOUBT. **After Burgoyne's force had been thrown back, the Americans pursued them, but were held up by the Balcarres Redoubt. As American reinforcements arrived, Arnold turned his attention to the Breymann Redoubt, which guarded the British right flank.**

Arnold galloped into the redoubt from the rear, but a grenadier shot him in the leg, and his horse was shot and fell. (As Arnold was pulled clear he prevented a soldier from killing the German.) At the same time, Breymann was killed (possibly by one of his own men), and German resistance crumbled.

regrouped. At this point, Arnold abandoned Poor and led Learned's right-hand regiments against the cabins, capturing them. He then charged into the redoubt, where his horse was shot down, and he broke the same leg he had injured at Quebec. With Morgan and Dearborn storming the front of the redoubt and their commander shot dead (possibly by one of his own men) the Germans fled.

As Learned's men carried Arnold from the field, more American units arrived (Paterson's brigade, a Massachusetts militia regiment, and three of Nixon's and Glover's units). Without a senior commander, they could do

The wounding of Simon Fraser, by S. Woodforde. **As the British line collapsed, both Arnold and Morgan recognized that Fraser was the only man capable of organizing further resistance, so they ordered riflemen to shoot him (something any British officer would have regarded as tantamount to murder). Shot through the stomach, by back-woodsman Tim Murphy (so legend has it) Fraser died the next morning after being tended by Riedesel's wife. He was buried, at his own request, in the Great Redoubt. (National Archives of Canada, C-46207)**

little except consolidate, but they knew that they had the key to Burgoyne's position (now manned by the 8th Massachusetts), and when 50 men under Lieutenant Colonel Speth tried to salvage German honor by retaking the redoubt under cover of darkness, they were promptly captured.

Burgoyne had suffered 894 casualties, including 278 killed:[2] Gates had lost around 200, of whom over 30 were dead. In all, some 4,000 Americans had participated in the main action, and as many more by the end of the day. That night, Burgoyne ordered a total withdrawal behind the Great Redoubt: as they dragged their cannon and baggage to the river, the British blamed everything on the Germans, and the Germans blamed everything on Burgoyne.

The retreat to Saratoga

Next morning, Lincoln and Glover scouted the British lines and reported that Burgoyne was withdrawing (as ever, confusion reigned in the dense forest – Lincoln mistakenly rode up to some Germans and received a leg wound that left him with a permanent limp), but Morgan and Dearborn, circling north, found no evidence of retreat. Gates sent more militia and artillery across the river to reinforce the New Hampshire and Massachusetts contingents massing at Saratoga. Meanwhile, American guns fired constantly, if fruitlessly, at the pontoon bridge, the British hospital, and at sunset, Simon Fraser's funeral cortège.

On October 8, Burgoyne finally agreed to retreat. Enemy movement on the east bank hastened the loading of the baggage train and bateaux, but over 300 sick were abandoned for lack of transport. At 21.00 Lieutenant Colonel Sutherland scouted the Saratoga road with the 47th and 9th, followed by Riedesel, the remaining Marksmen and Indians, then Burgoyne with Hamilton and the baggage. Phillips, now commanding the Advance Corps, brought up the rear, and the Loyalists took the 47th's place in the bateaux, rowing upstream against a heavy current.

Almost immediately, torrential rain fell, turning the road into a quagmire and hindering reconstruction of the bridges destroyed by the militia. The rearguard did not depart until 04.00 on October 9, breaking the bridges behind them, and when the front of the column halted to eat an hour later, it had covered less than five miles. The halt lasted ten hours, with Burgoyne hoping Gates would attack in the rain, allowing cannon and bayonets to decide the day. As his men stood in the rain, Burgoyne found a warm cabin, where he signed a pass allowing the pregnant Harriet Acland to join her captured husband.

Meanwhile Sutherland found Fellows' entire brigade asleep in their camp, but Burgoyne decided he was too weak to attack. At 16.00 the army moved off again (Fellows, alerted by Gates, having fallen back to the east bank) but the weather forced Burgoyne to abandon his baggage and the Americans found dead horses, wrecked carts, and supplies all over the road, the rain having thwarted all attempts to burn anything useful. It was

Looking east towards the Bloody Knoll. **As Poor chased the British rearguard, he overran the defensive work on a rocky outcrop (at right, marked by white posts), later known as the 'Bloody Knoll'. This served as a warning post for the Balcarres Redoubt, covering a gully that would otherwise have provided 'dead ground' for any attacker. (Author's photograph)**

TOP *Looking east towards the Balcarres Redoubt.* **Having overrun the 'Bloody Knoll', Poor suddenly found himself confronted by the Balcarres Redoubt – between 12 and 14 feet high, built of logs covered in earth, mounting eight cannon, and protected by a strong abattis. It was manned by the British light infantry and the survivors of the morning's advance. (Author's photograph)**

ABOVE *Looking west from the Balcarres Redoubt.* **The defenders' view of the ground Poor's brigade covered in its series of attacks. In the center, some 200 yards away, is the 'Bloody Knoll'. (Author's photograph)**

dark when the column reached Fish Kill: the Germans and the Advance Corps waded across, but the guns had to be left due to the water level and the condition of the horses.

Next day, the British contingent (including the artillery) crossed. With the militia massing on the east bank, Burgoyne decided to stay on the west until Fort Edward. Sutherland went ahead with the 47th, Marksmen, Canadians, and artificers to scout the road and repair the bridges, while the main body stayed in Saratoga. Around 11.00, with enemy patrols now appearing to the west and south, Burgoyne had Schuyler's house burned to clear his field of fire, and recalled Sutherland.

Gates had been caught napping and initially had seemed happy to let Burgoyne go. With Arnold and Lincoln out of action, he now had to command eight brigades on the west bank and co-ordinate six others (all militia) on the east bank. Finally he advanced on October 10, rapidly overtaking Burgoyne and reaching the Fish Kill around 16.00, just as militia units attacked Sutherland and forced him to withdraw.

Burgoyne now dug in, still harboring dreams of his guns catching Gates in the open. The troops worked throughout the night to improve the light defenses constructed during their advance (and those built by Fellows later). The cold, stony ground made it noisy work, but it went unreported by American sentries and, as Fellows had informed Gates of Sutherland leaving but not returning, Gates assumed Burgoyne was still moving north. Expecting to find only a rearguard, he ordered a general advance across the Fish Kill at first light, without any reconnaissance.

October 11 dawned thick and foggy as Glover, Learned, and Nixon crossed the stream and started up the slopes toward 27 British guns. An advance party of 50 of Nixon's men took a 36-man British picket without a shot. However, a deserter warned Glover of the trap, and he and Nixon halted while Gates was informed: Learned continued but was stopped by orders from Gates. Suddenly, the fog lifted and the British artillery opened fire as the Americans scrambled out of range. Later Learned, Poor, and Paterson, with several guns, joined Morgan and Dearborn (who had earlier

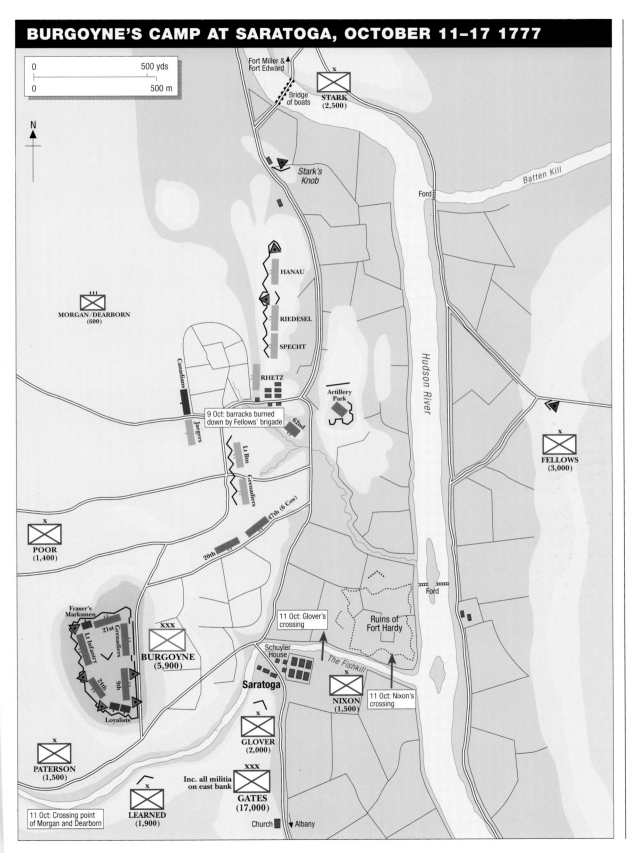

BURGOYNE'S CAMP AT SARATOGA, OCTOBER 11–17 1777

0   500 yds

0   500 m

N

Fort Miller &
Fort Edward

Bridge
of boats

STARK
(2,500)

Stark's
Knob

Batten Kill

Ford

HANAU

MORGAN/DEARBORN
(600)

RIEDESEL

SPECHT

Hudson River

Canadians

RHETZ

Artillery
Park

Jaegers

9 Oct: barracks burned
down by Fellows' brigade

62nd

Lt Bn

Grenadiers

x
FELLOWS
(3,000)

x
POOR
(1,400)

47th (6 Cos)

20th

Ford

11 Oct: Glover's
crossing

Ruins of
Fort Hardy

Fraser's
Marksmen

21st Grenadiers

Lt Infantry

xxx
BURGOYNE
(5,900)

11 Oct: Nixon's
crossing

24th

9th

Schuyler
House

The Fishkill

x
NIXON
(1,500)

Loyalists

Saratoga

x
PATERSON
(1,500)

x
GLOVER
(2,000)

Inc. all militia
on east bank

xxx
GATES
(17,000)

11 Oct: Crossing point
of Morgan and Dearborn

x
LEARNED
(1,900)

Church ■ ▼ Albany

TOP *Looking south-east towards the Breymann Redoubt.* **This is the view from the knoll defended by the Jaegers on October 7. It shows the north end of the main work (the grassy mound at left was a smaller work, facing north to protect the main redoubt's flank and rear). The redoubt was in fact a palisade of horizontally laid logs, with firing slits and several right-angled sally-ports to allow the garrison to form in front. (Author's photograph)**

moved around the edge of the bluffs and found themselves above the fog looking down on the British camp) on the heights west of Burgoyne's position.

American artillery and riflemen now began firing on the camp from several points, causing many casualties; raiding parties captured several bateaux, forcing the British to haul the remaining cargoes into their lines; and a 50-strong German picket deserted *en masse*. That evening Burgoyne, Phillips, Riedesel, and Hamilton met to consider their options: await an attack; attack themselves; retreat with the artillery and baggage; retreat without them; or march south to Albany. With all but the fourth deemed impracticable, they resolved to leave that night: unfortunately, there were now too many enemy patrols for even this plan to succeed. Frustrated, Burgoyne turned on Skene, demanding advice. Skene told Burgoyne that if he scattered his baggage and stores along the route, the militia would be too busy plundering to fight him.

The Convention Army

Reduced to 3,500 effectives, Burgoyne called another council of war on October 14 to discuss whether capitulation would be honorable. Every officer above captain attended and unanimously agreed that it was, so Major Kingston, was sent to Gates under a flag of truce (he was also blind-folded). To his astonishment, on presenting Burgoyne's offer to negotiate,

Gates produced a pre-written letter demanding total surrender (possibly a bluff, driven by fear that Clinton's arrival would trap him). An armistice was agreed until sunset, then extended until 10.00 on October 15.

A second letter from Gates stipulated a capitulation at 15.00 that day, with all arms laid down by 17.00. This preciseness made Burgoyne suspicious – perhaps Clinton was near and Gates knew. He played for time, demanding the full honors of war, adding that his men would sooner 'rush on the enemy determined to take no quarter' than be disarmed in camp. He also insisted that his army be returned to England, on condition they did not serve in North America again. Gates agreed at once, and Sutherland and Captain Craig of the 47th met Lieutenant Colonel Wilkinson and Brigadier General Whipple to draft the terms.

That night Sutherland and Craig presented the treaty to Burgoyne, who accepted, subject to replacing 'capitulation' with 'convention'. Craig wrote to Wilkinson, stating Burgoyne's acceptance and condition, and Gates, having just heard that Clinton had captured the Highland forts, agreed at once. The same news reached Burgoyne the next day and he reconvened his council of war to discuss whether he was bound by the treaty, or whether he could act on the news (and if so, whether his army would actually fight).

The answer was no: 14 of the 22 officers felt that he was bound by the treaty, and Clinton was in any event too far away: more felt that the troops

BELOW *Looking west and south-west from the Breymann Redoubt.* **This view shows the sheer size of the redoubt which, following the earlier debacle, was held by only 200 men. Just right of center is the knoll on which there was a square earthwork manned by the Jaegers; the center and left saw the first attacks by Learned and Morgan. Arnold's attack broke in at the far left. (Author's photograph)**

would not do well if forced to fight. Burgoyne played for time, accusing Gates of sending troops to Albany in contravention of the treaty (in fact they were time-expired militiamen marching home without orders) and demanded to count his men. Wilkinson denied the accusation and threatened to cease negotiations: as he rode away, Kingston caught up with him and promised an answer within two hours.

Burgoyne again conferred: Phillips had no advice to offer, while Riedesel and Hamilton felt that refuting the agreement would be hazardous. However, Burgoyne was determined, and sent Sutherland to inform Wilkinson the truce had ended. The choice was fortuitous:[3] during their conversation, Sutherland saw Craig's letter for the first time: realizing its implications, he took it to Burgoyne who agreed that he was irrevocably committed and signed.

At 10.00 on October 17 the troops marched out with the honors of war to ground their arms by the river and begin the 200-mile walk to Boston (except the Canadians, who returned to Canada, and the Loyalists who had slipped away during the armistice). At noon, Burgoyne and his senior officers gathered outside a marquee, presented their swords to Gates, and were invited to dinner: later, as they watched Gates' troops march south, both British and German officers remarked on their enemies' military bearing and good order. Burgoyne was given a cavalry escort to Albany, where he was entertained by Schuyler. Of almost 10,000 who left St John's in June, 5,895 remained – 3,018 British, 2,412 Germans and 465 'auxiliaries' – plus 215 British and 82 German women, an assortment of camp followers, and a menagerie of local wildlife adopted by the Germans. Some 1,728 men had been killed or captured; 1,297 remained at Ticonderoga (till November 8, when they withdrew to Canada, having destroyed the fortifications); the remainder had either deserted, or – like their leader – had become 'lost in the wilderness'.

On October 15, after receiving reinforcements, Vaughan continued up river to see if he could either contact Burgoyne or supply him via the Hudson. Putnam, bolstered by 1,200 Connecticut and 1,000 New Jersey militia, was content to observe; the Clinton brothers were more aggressive, ordering out the militia, while Gates sent the 1st New York from Fort Schuyler and several hundred of his Albany and Connecticut militia.

The next day, Vaughan reached Esopus (burning it to prevent the garrison cutting his communications with Fort Clinton) and Livingston's Manor, which was 45 miles from Albany and barely 70 from Burgoyne. Unfortunately Wallace's pilots refused to continue, and attempts to contact Burgoyne proved fruitless – though information on his plight was all too readily obtained. Facing Putnam's 5,000 men on the east bank and another 1,500 – along with Gates' army – on the west, Vaughan withdrew to New York City on October 17.

Footnotes

1 One grenadier company lost 16 out of 21 all ranks: Acland, shot through both legs, had to be saved from being killed by a boy.

2 British losses were 31 officers and 600 men (184 dead, 264 wounded, and 183 captured); German losses numbered 263 (94 dead, 67 wounded, and 102 captured).

3 It later transpired that the Americans had intended to give no quarter.

AFTERMATH

Escorted by Glover's brigade, Burgoyne's force – now known as the Convention Army – arrived in Cambridge on November 6. The men entered rough barracks on Prospect and Winter hills: the officers (save for three from each regiment in the barracks) were billeted in the town. However, food and conditions were so poor that Burgoyne – who had advanced £20,000 of his own money for his men's welfare – wrote to Gates, complaining 'the public faith is broke'.

Staggered by Gates' largesse and aware of the implications of the treaty, Congress – including members who understood Gates' lack of options – lost no time seeking ways to circumvent it. The surrender of only 648 cartridge boxes and Burgoyne's failure to supply descriptions of every man (to identify them if they did return) were chosen, until something more substantial appeared, as it duly did. Congress seized on Burgoyne's letter: if the British felt Congress had broken faith, they would no longer feel bound themselves. And with insufficient ships and provisions for a transatlantic voyage, surely they had to keep the troops in America? In December, ships sent to collect the troops were barred from Boston harbor. (Unbeknown to Congress, Howe did plan to use the men in America, but to exchange them for American prisoners, as permitted under Article 3 of the Convention.)

On January 3 1778 Congress resolved to detain the Convention Army until the British government ratified the treaty – knowing full well that this would by implication be recognition of American independence and that the King would prevent it. (In fact, the King did order Clinton to ratify it, whereupon Congress, claiming the order was forged, requested a witness to the King's signature!) Burgoyne and two aides were allowed home in April, but the rest of the Convention Army stayed in captivity, moving – usually in mid-winter – from Massachusetts to Virginia (many of the Germans 'disappearing' en route as Congress had hoped), and later to Maryland, before being split up to prevent Cornwallis rescuing them. Barely half of the rank-and-file were released at the end of the war, the rest having either deserted, escaped, or died from cold or hunger. From 1779, officers were gradually released on parole, but even Phillips and Riedesel were not exchanged until late 1780.

Opinion in Europe

Word of Saratoga reached Paris on December 5 1777 – rather fortuitously, as the abandonment of Fort Ticonderoga and the loss of Philadelphia had damaged the American cause. King Louis XVI declared his recognition of the United States of America the next day. Yet despite celebrating Gates' victory as if it had been theirs, many in France feared that overt support might backfire if a reconciliation occurred – an outcome that, for different reasons, both the Americans and the British suggested might be increasingly likely. However, having just agreed proposals for naval operations against the West Indies, Louis and his foreign secretary, the Comte de Vergennes, decided to meet Franklin, and a formal treaty of alliance was signed on February 6 1778.

The effect in Britain

London learned of Burgoyne's defeat when a letter from Carleton arrived on December 3. Burgoyne's official dispatch, carried by Lord Petersham, reached England on December 15 (with a secret copy for the Earl of Derby in case Germain censored the original). Denied a court of enquiry, Burgoyne presented his case in the House of Commons, condemning Germain's orders as too precise: Howe did the same, complaining that they were too vague! Public opinion favored Burgoyne (blaming Howe or Germain, according to political leaning) but in truth, all three had made mistakes in promoting – or failing to prevent – a plan that was infeasible, given the lack of manpower and inherent logistical difficulties.

Despite his claims to have been depending on Howe, Burgoyne had boasted that he would reach Albany unaided and await Howe's arrival (and indeed, this had been his plan, to avoid sharing any glory). Germain, though guilty *ex post facto* of half-truths and of withholding vital correspondence from public scrutiny, may, given his ignorance of the geography of North America, have believed that the plans he had approved were complementary, rather than contradictory. Where he undoubtedly did err was in sending Howe a copy of Burgoyne's plan rather than specific orders relating to it.

Technically, Howe had done no wrong: he had warned Carleton against expecting aid from himself and delayed his move against Philadelphia until Burgoyne's optimistic letter of July 11. He had seen Washington as the one real threat to Burgoyne and one which he could have negated by following if Washington did move north. He had felt that Clinton had enough men to support Burgoyne against lesser forces. Charged (perhaps rightly) with indifference to Burgoyne's fate, he emphasized the likely losses from assaulting the Highland forts with Washington's army supporting them, and added – with justification – that had he aided Burgoyne, his political foes would have accused him of stealing the latter's glory and wasting the campaigning season. (Interestingly, Burgoyne never challenged Howe's statement, and the two remained friends.) For his part, Clinton agreed with Howe's assessment of Burgoyne's chances. His subsequent protest to Germain that Howe's plan to attack Philadelphia had left him too weak to defend New York City and aid Burgoyne also negates the argument that Howe ignored the Government's wishes.

Saratoga was a watershed: the first time British regulars were beaten in open battle by equal numbers of Americans. Moreover, the Continentals had borne the brunt of the fighting, supported by 'hordes' of militia who had proved adept at attacking detachments or lines of communication. Expectations that Loyalists would swell British numbers, or take control of subjugated areas, had proved groundless. (Ironically, the transfer of 5,000 troops to defend the West Indies against the French subsequently made such expectations a cornerstone of British strategy.) And as so often throughout the war, the weather had favored the Americans: a late thaw had delayed Burgoyne, while rain had saved Herkimer, held up Breymann, and sabotaged the retreat.

Defeat cost Great Britain more than an army (which it could, with difficulty, replace). The after-shock in America (on both sides) and Europe transformed a civil war into a global struggle against the two colonial superpowers of the day, France and Spain, and eventually lost George III his American colonies.

CHRONOLOGY

The course of the war, 1775–77

1775

April 19 – Lexington and Concord
April 20 (to March 17 1776) – Siege of Boston
May 10-12 – Capture of Ticonderoga and Crown Point
June 16 – Washington appointed commander-in-chief of Continental Army
June 17 – Battle of Bunker's Hill
June 25 – Schuyler appointed commander of Northern Department
August 28 (to June 14 1776) – American invasion of Canada
December 2 (to May 6 1776) – Siege of Quebec
December 9 – Dunmore defeated at Great Bridge, Virginia

1776

January 2 – Burning of Norfolk, Virginia
January 17 – Schuyler captures Johnson Hall, New York
February 27 – Loyalists defeated at Moore's Creek Bridge, North Carolina
April 13 – Washington organizes defenses of New York City
June 8 – American defeat at Trois Rivières
June 28 – British repulse at Charleston, South Carolina
July 3 – British occupy Staten Island
July 4 – Declaration of Independence
July 7 – Survivors of Canadian expedition arrive at Crown Point
July 9 to August 1 – British forces concentrate off Long Island
August 22 to November 20 – New York campaign
September 21 – New York City fire
October 11/12 – Carleton defeats Arnold at Valcour Island (Lake Champlain)
October 14 – Americans burn and abandon Crown Point
November 4 – Winter forces Carleton back to Canada
November 21 – December 14 – Washington flees across New Jersey
December 8 – British capture Newport, Rhode Island
December 25/26 – American victory at Trenton

1777

January 3/4 – American victory at Princeton
June 12-26 – Howe fails to trap Washington in New Jersey

The Campaign, May 6–October 17

May 6 – Burgoyne arrives at Quebec from England
June 12 – St Clair takes command at Ticonderoga
June 13 – Main British force sets off down Lake Champlain
June 23 – St Leger leaves Montreal for Oswego
June 25 – Burgoyne's advance guard occupies Crown Point
July 2-4 – Burgoyne's army invests Ticonderoga
July 5 – British guns spotted on Mount Defiance
July 6 – St Clair abandons Ticonderoga and Mount Independence
July 7 – Action at Hubbardton, Vermont
July 8 – General Howe's army embarks for Philadelphia
July 9 – Action near Fort Ann, New York
July 9-27 – Burgoyne's army clears a passage to Fort Ann
July 17 – New Hampshire raises militia force under Stark
July 23 – The Howes set sail from New York City
July 25 – St Leger arrives at Oswego
July 29 – Schuyler abandons Fort Edward
August 2/3 – St Leger's force arrives at Fort Stanwix
August 6 – Battle of Oriskany
August 10 – Schuyler sends Arnold to relieve Fort Stanwix
August 11 – Burgoyne despatches Baum's column
August 14 – Congress orders Gates to replace Schuyler
August 15 – Burgoyne despatches Breymann's column
August 16 – Battle of Bennington
19 August – Gates joins Northern Army at Stillwater
August 22 – St Leger abandons siege
August 25 – General Howe disembarks at Head of Elk
August 28 – December 11 – Philadelphia campaign
September 11 – Battle of Brandywine Creek, Pennsylvania
September 12 – Americans fortify Bemis Heights
September 13 – Burgoyne crosses to west bank of Hudson
September 15-18 – American attacks on Diamond Island and Ticonderoga
September 19 – First battle of Saratoga (Freeman's Farm)
September 20/21 – Paoli 'massacre'
September 23 – General Howe occupies Philadelphia

October 3 – Clinton sets out to join Burgoyne

October 4 – Battle of Germantown, Pennsylvania

October 6 – Capture of Forts Montgomery and Clinton

October 7 – Second battle of Saratoga (Bemis Heights)

October 9-11 – Burgoyne's army withdraws to Saratoga

October 12 – Gates surrounds Burgoyne

October 13-16 – Burgoyne negotiates with Gates

October 16 – Vaughan burns Esopus

October 17 – Convention Army leaves Saratoga: Vaughan returns to New York City

October 22 – Vaughan abandons Fort Montgomery

October 22/23 – Americans repel assaults on Forts Mercer and Mifflin, Pennsylvania

November 6 – Convention Army arrives in Cambridge, Massachusetts

November 8 – Powell destroys Fort Ticonderoga and retreats to Canada

November 15-20 – Americans abandon Forts Mifflin and Mercer

December 19 – Washington's Main Army arrives at Valley Forge for the winter

December 23 – Ships refused entry to Boston to take Convention Army home

Aftermath, 1778–1783

January 3 1778 – Congress demands ratification of Convention

February 6 1778 – France signs treaty of alliance

March 13 1778 – France declares war on Great Britain

April 5 1778 – Burgoyne leaves for England

January/February 1779 – Convention Army moved to Charlottesville, Virginia

November 1779 – Phillips paroled, returns to New York City

October 1780 – Phillips and Riedesel exchanged for Lincoln

June/July 1781 – Convention Army split up to prevent rescue by Cornwallis

April 1783 – Congress releases remaining 2,500 rank-and-file

A GUIDE TO FURTHER READING

In addition to the general works listed in Campaign 37 *Boston 1775* and Campaign 47 *Yorktown 1781*, the following relate directly to this campaign.

On the commanders: Mintz, M. M. *The Generals of Saratoga* (Yale 1990); Lunt, J. *John Burgoyne of Saratoga* (London 1976). On the American side: Rossie, J.G. *The Politics of Command in the American Revolution* (New York 1975) reviews Congressional military appointments; Gerlach, D.R. *Proud Patriot* (New York 1987) portrays Schuyler's life; while Randall, W.S. *Benedict Arnold, Patriot and Traitor* (New York 1990) and Brandt, C. *The Man in the Mirror* (New York 1994) discuss Arnold's life. For the remainder: Boatner, M. *Biographical Dictionary of the American War of Independence* (London 1974); *Dictionary of National Biography* (London 1901); and Purcell, L.E. *Who was Who in the American Revolution* (New York 1993).

On the armies: Rogers, H. *Lieutenant Hadden's Journal and Orderly Books* (New York 1884); Baxter, J.P. *The British Invasion from the North, with the Journal of Lieutenant William Digby* (New York 1887); and Anburey, T. *Travels through the interior parts of North America* (New York 1969) – widely regarded as plagiarism.

On Tories: Van Tyne, C.H. *The Loyalists in the American Revolution* (Bowie, MD 1989); and Ranlet, R. *The New York Loyalists* (Knoxville, TN 1986).

On the Brunswick and Hesse-Hanau troops: Stone, W.L. (trans.) *Memoir,. Letters and Journals of Major General Riedesel* (New York 1969); *Journal of Captain Pausch* (New York 1971); Doblin, H. (trans.) *Journal of J. F. Wasmus, German Company Surgeon, 1776-1783* (Westport, CT 1990); and *Journal of an officer in the Prinz Friedrich Regiment, 1776-1783* (Westport, CT 1993). For insight into the Continentals: Neimeyer, C.P. *America goes to war* (New York 1996); Royster, C. *A Revolutionary People at War* (North Carolina 1979); and Baldwin, J. *The Revolutionary Journal of Colonel Jeduthan Baldwin* (New York 1971).

Elting, J.R. *The Battles of Saratoga* (New Jersey 1977) displays soldierly insight and exposes several myths; Ketchum, R.M. Saratoga, *Turning Point of America's Revolutionary War* (New York 1997) and Furneaux, R. *Saratoga: the Decisive Battle* (London 1971) describe the campaign from journals and diaries. Pancake, J. S. *The Year of the Hangman* (London 1992) covers Clinton in the Hudson Highlands. Williams, J. *The Battle of Hubbardton* (Vermont 1988) and Lord, P. *War over Walloomscoick* (New York 1989) are good local histories. Scott, A.J. *Fort Stanwix and Oriskany* (New York 1927) describes St Leger's expedition. On the Convention Army: Dabney, W.M. *After Saratoga: The Story of the Convention Army* (New York 1954).

Finally, Burgoyne, J. *A State of the Expedition from Canada* (London 1780) and Clinton, Sir H. *The American Rebellion* (New Haven 1954) (ed. Wilcox, W.B.) – read neither in isolation!

Maps and charts: Marshall, W. and Peckham, H. *Campaigns of the American Revolution* (New Jersey 1976); and Symonds, C. and Clipson, W. *A Battlefield Atlas of the American Revolution* (Annapolis 1986).

Orders-of-battle were gleaned from Public Records Office, Kew, England; the works above; and Novak, G. *We have always governed ourselves* (Champaign 1990).

WARGAMING THE SARATOGA CAMPAIGN

What makes the American Revolution particularly suited to wargaming is the limited number of men involved, especially compared with other 'horse-and-musket' conflicts. This allows low figure-to-man ratios and realistic ground scales, thus accurately recreating the problems historical commanders faced in moving formed bodies of men. Other factors specific to the Saratoga campaign include the effect of the terrain on logistics and the gradual improvement in the performance of the Continentals, who for the first time outfought British regulars in the later battles, after a lackluster start to the campaign. The outcome might have been different had Burgoyne pressed harder in July and August and not allowed Schuyler to regroup.

The capture of Fort Ticonderoga

At first sight, this event seems unworthy of a refight, but short role-playing or skirmish games can be based on American patroling against the British Advance Corps and Indians at Crown Point in late June, or the initial 'rush' on July 2. Still more interesting is to consider how a siege might have evolved. How long would Burgoyne have bombarded before assaulting the fort? What would his losses have been? Equally, how long could St Clair have held out – or been forced to by his men – before surrendering, or trying to escape (especially with Riedesel cutting off his retreat)? This would make a fascinating 'committee' game, with players role-playing St Clair and his subordinates, and an umpire controlling events and the enemy. Each player's agenda will determine his support for St Clair (or not) and, as a nod to realism, de Rochefermoy's objectives might include drinking a prescribed amount of alcohol!

If a figure game is desired, use two tables, one for each Fort, linked – notionally, at least – by the boat bridge, which the British can destroy only after they breach the boom. Either garrison may support the other while the bridge is intact, though personality clashes (and the lower chance of escape from Ticonderoga) may affect this. As a change from commercial rules, use 'kriegsspiel' and the wargames section in Christopher Duffy's *Fire and Stone* (which exposes the myth that sieges were mathematically predictable).[1]

Hubbardton

This classic rearguard action, involving 2,000 men on a field some 2,000 yards square (if all three American defensive lines are included), could easily be refought at 1:1 in 1/300, while offering a rare chance for maneuver without the table edge becoming a defensive aid. Victory conditions – based on how many Americans escape and how much the British pursuit of St Clair is delayed – are obvious; Hale's stragglers can disrupt both sides; and a multi-player defense can reflect friction between Francis and Warner. 'Randomizing' Riedesel's arrival keeps the British player guessing while offering the Americans the chance to counter-attack – or over-extend!

Fort Stanwix and Oriskany

With neither the firepower nor the manpower to storm Fort Stanwix, and insufficient time to starve it into surrender, St Leger's only hope (short of the traditional lucky hit on a magazine) was to destroy the garrison's morale, partly through constant sniping and bombardment, but mainly by killing any hope of relief. Since this makes a very tedious game, the answer is either to play one side solo – preferably with an umpire – and/or a simple 'pencil-and-paper' exercise (e.g. an amended version of Jim Webster's 'Firebase Defence' in *Miniature Wargames* 35) to recreate the 'quiet' periods. Repeated false (and occasional genuine) alarms will sap the garrison's morale, diminishing its ability to repel an assault or making surrender more appealing (successful sorties have the opposite effect). By concealing the exact level of deterioration (with an umpire) or only calculating it at the last minute (without one), the player estimates his chances of a successful assault (or defense). Players should also allow for demoralization among the Iroquois.

The terrain for Oriskany is probably too difficult to recreate in a practicable form, but specific incidents – the attack on the rearguard, the rally on the knoll, or the attempted Tory deception – make ideal skirmishes (with or without role-play). Alternatively, both sides can be scaled down to *Brother Against Brother* dimensions, or players can adapt Andy Callan's 'Forest Fight' rules (*The Nugget*). Again, the Iroquois require special rules for 'triggering' the ambush too soon, chasing fugitives instead of attacking the main body, and losing heart after modest losses. A 'what-if' option can pitch St Leger (with or without the Iroquois) against Arnold's relief force.

Burgoyne's Road and Bennington

Schuyler's 'scorched earth' policy suggests a role-playing game, with victory points for 'creative vandalism' on one side, and ingenious solutions on the other, while attacks on British working parties offer endless skirmish scenarios, either as 'one-off' games or within a map-based game, such as L.J. Watts' 'Maroon' (*Miniature Wargames* 29).

Baum's foraging expedition also suggests a map-game, with added role-play elements – namely language problems and differing political agenda for the Loyalists and Indians. The militia who 'shadowed' Baum until Stark's arrival can be generated using systems such as that in *Pony Wars*. The battle could be refought on one table, but given the poor lines of sight between Baum's positions, it might be more interesting as a series of games – the bridge, the redoubt, the jaeger picket, and Breymann's arrival (a useful variable or 'what if') – in separate rooms or behind screens.

Freeman's Farm and Bemis Heights

The common factor in these two battles is that the terrain conveniently split them into several smaller actions, mostly fought out of sight of one another. This offers a rare opportunity to have tabletop commanders genuinely looking over their shoulder(s) to see who (or what) might be behind them. In both instances, any rules used must emphasize the problems of maintaining unit cohesion in difficult terrain and the effects on command and control of officers being picked off by riflemen.

Freeman's Farm offers an interesting skirmish game, based on Morgan's ambush and subsequent repulse, as a prelude to a normal figure game. Intervention by Fraser or Riedesel (or even Gates along the river road) can be introduced to provide more suspense. The second battle is best fought as a series of smaller clashes, starting with Morgan and Dearborn's attack.

Elsewhere, a mini-campaign could be based around the militia attacks on Fort Ticonderoga and Lake George. There are also opportunities for committee/role-play games recreating the various councils of war, particularly among Burgoyne's senior officers, throughout September and October, and a map game based on the retreat, with points for each element of the army which evades capture and reaches Ticonderoga. On the other side, the Gates-Arnold conflict offers opportunities for robust role-play; and a 'what if' game can be based on the 'Fog on the Fish Kill' incident of October 10.

Finally, role-playing and figure gaming can be combined in following one unit's fortunes on the battlefield (mainly through the eyes of its officers) by adapting Arthur Harman's 'Hard Pounding' and 'Sawbones' (*Miniature Wargames* 45 and 46), themselves based on John Keegan's *Face of Battle*. Using a 1:1 ratio, the figures remain in the center of the table (which need not be large), while 'rolling' scenery reflects movement. Obvious examples are the 9th at Fort Ann, the 62nd at Freeman's Farm, or one of Poor's units in either of the main actions.

The Hudson Highlands

The only action of note (pace putative pyromaniacs wishing to recreate the burning of Esopus) was the storming of the forts. Given the British need to move rapidly (and the lack of heavy artillery) a 'storming' game is the obvious option, though the Clintons' escape might make a role-playing exercise (as would Putnam's antics). An interesting 'what if' is to see how far Vaughan can go up-river and decide to challenge the gathering rebel forces.

Campaign or 'map' games

The entire campaign can easily be refought on relief maps – the United States Geological Survey (USGS) in Denver provides state maps to 1:25,000 (about 2.5 inches to the mile), and similar material is increasingly becoming available in computer packages. Obviously these are modern maps, but judicious copying and deleting can retain natural features and restore man-made ones to their historical limits.

Although the upper New York area is large, the action – Bennington apart – centered on the two river valleys. The vital aspect is Burgoyne's supply problem. The campaign was unique, not only in the Americans having better access to supplies, but also in their having better administrators. Gates and Schuyler kept their troops far better fed (admittedly in easier circumstances) than did Burgoyne, whose logistical problems not only dictated his strategy, but forced increasingly desperate gambles on him. (Many 'expert' wargamers might benefit from having to feed 7,000 men in such a wilderness!)

Other factors to consider include the effect of Indians both on American morale and on Burgoyne's ability to 'screen' his army (especially once they start to leave); the improvement in the performance and morale of the Continentals – and a similar degradation in that of the British and German troops, as losses mount and supplies run low; and the generation of militia, whether local units turning out to defend their homes, or those levied specifically to serve with the Northern Army. In Europe, around 10 per cent of the population would be men of military age (15 to 50): as a frontier colony, New York probably had fewer women and children and more men with military experience – perhaps 20,000. Given Loyalist numbers and the threats to the Mohawk and lower Hudson, probably only 10,000 at most were available to serve with the main armies, with another 10,000 – including 50-60 year-olds – available for 'local' defense across the colony.

A final word on rules
In reality, every battle is different and unless one side is substantially superior 'local' differences often determine the outcome. Rules should therefore be minimal at the general level, concentrating on mechanics, but become more detailed in relation to a specific action or series of actions with similar circumstances and results. Many of the above ideas involve players making up the rules as they go, to a greater or lesser extent. Reproducing the main actions of the Saratoga campaign is beyond most commercial rules – even those 'designed' for this conflict which are often only thinly-disguised Frederician or Napoleonic sets that leave players refighting even the biggest battles with a handful of three- or four-figure units. This 'tokenism' turns figure games into boardgames and defeats the object of having figures – at least counters can carry data!

In fact, the Saratoga actions require so many 'local' rules that players may as well write their own, though having said that, commercial rules for the French and Indian Wars, being designed mainly for skirmishes (e.g. *Ranger* by Peter Berry, or *Brother against Brother*, although the squad tended to be an administrative rather than a tactical unit in this period) provide a good starting point. Simplifying the 'four Ms' – musketry, melée, movement and morale – will raise the level to company or regimental actions, but keep paperwork to acceptable levels and allow players to recreate North American warfare, rather than European warfare transported to North America.

Footnote

1 This misconception (identified by Duffy) stems from a misreading of Vauban's calculation of how many days' supplies his citadel at Lille would require to withstand a full-blown siege. It has since been cited repeatedly – by soldiers, historians, and wargamers – as evidence that the fall of a defensive work could be calculated according to a precise timetable of activity (something Vauban would probably have regarded as nonsense).

VISITING THE
BATTLEFIELDS TODAY

The Saratoga campaign occurred over a large area, so a car is essential for visiting the main sites. Look out for the roadside plaques (dark blue with yellow text) indicating sites of historic interest, but be aware that the subject may no longer exist, or may now be private property. Also, remember to check the opening times of major sites in advance. (Many open on Sunday, but close on Mondays – except when Monday is a public holiday.) Restoration work may also curtail access.

Crown Point

DIRECTIONS: Crown Point can be reached via I-87 (J28), then east on NY-74 to the intersection with NY-22 (or 9N). Follow NY-22 north to NY-17, then four miles beyond the village to Lake Champlain bridge.

DETAILS: A visitor center gives the history of both forts (the other being Fort St Frédéric); to the west is where Burgoyne's army assembled in June 1777.

Fort Ticonderoga

ADDRESS:

Fort Ticonderoga
PO Box 390
Ticonderoga, NY 12883

DIRECTIONS: Fort Ticonderoga can be reached via I-87 (J28), then east on NY-74 to the intersection with NY-22 (or 9N). Head south on NY-22, then east on NY-74 at the second intersection.

DETAILS: Visitors enter the garrison grounds through iron gates, and drive through the Carillon Battlefield, the site of the greatest French victory of the Seven Years War as well as the subsequent battles during the French and Indian and American Revolutionary wars. A half mile down the road lie 'the French Lines', earthworks thrown up by desperate French troops in July 1758, where a French force of 3,000 men held off a British attack by 15,000 soldiers in the Battle of Carillon. On the left side of the road just outside the French

defenses is a memorial cairn commemorating the valor of the Black Watch regiment: across the road is a replica of the wooden cross erected by the Marquis de Montcalm giving thanks to God for the French victory against overwhelming odds.

A half mile farther the woods give way to open fields, good views of Lake Champlain, then a picnic area, and Fort Ticonderoga just ahead.

The Log House welcomes visitors with signage in both French and English: self-guiding brochures in French or English also are available. Admission tickets are sold here (Canadian dollars accepted at par for admission). There is a bookshop for titles on 18th-century military matters and colonial life, a souvenir shop, and a restaurant.

Throughout the day guided tours begin at the flag bastion, led by men and women uniformed in period dress. Weather permitting there are also musket or artillery demonstrations.

Staff are on hand to talk about the exhibits of 18th-century arms, accoutrements, personal effects of soldiers, paintings and maps. Visitors also find chronological exhibits of the history of the Ticonderoga peninsula, beginning with the Native American occupation 10,000 years ago, Samuel de Champlain's visit in 1609, the building of the Fort in 1755, the campaigns of the French and Indian War and the American Revolution, and the restoration of the Fort beginning in 1909. There is also a room devoted to a famous namesake of the Fort, the USS *Ticonderoga*, the World War 2 aircraft carrier. The largest collection of 18th-century cannon in the Western Hemisphere is mounted on the curtain walls of the Fort. Throughout the season reenactors portraying historic regiments visit Ticonderoga and set up period camps. Readers may be particularly interested in the Revolutionary War Encampment held the weekend following Labor Day. You can also learn about another side of the Fort Ticonderoga story by entering the world of the Native peoples who lived here for thousands of years prior to European contact and then fought as allies of the British, French and American forces during the 18th-century wars in the Lake Champlain and Lake George valleys.

Visitors can also drive to the summit of Mount Defiance, where General Burgoyne's cannon forced the evacuation of the Fort a year and a day after the Americans had declared independence.

OPENING AND ADMISSIONS: Fort Ticonderoga is open daily from early May through the end of October. Hours are 9.00 to 17.00, seven days; the Fort is open until 18.00 during July and August. There is an admission charge, but children under seven enter for free.

WEBSITE: For more details on the fort, visit www.fort-ticonderoga.org

Mount Independence

DIRECTIONS: Mount Independence is in Vermont, and is best reached by the local ferry. If coming from Fort Ticonderoga, head east on NY-74. On the Vermont side, follow VT-74 to the intersection with VT-73, then head south-east for five miles, and just before the intersection with VT-22A, turn right onto a minor road (signposted) for another five miles.

DETAILS: The fortifications on Mount Independence are preserved jointly by the Fort Ticonderoga Association and the Vermont Division for Historic Preservation. The 400-acre site has a visitor center and is covered by color-coded trails (red is the quickest and shortest).

Hubbardton

DIRECTIONS: For Hubbardton, from the north, take VT-73, then south on VT-30, and left onto Monument Road (a dirt track in some places), six miles beyond Sudbury; from the south, take US-7 and join US-4 just south of Rutland, then turn right (J5) onto Monument Road.

DETAILS: The visitor center has an interactive map that shows the various stages of the battle. Zion Hill and Sucker Brook are on private land, but the steepness of the ground Fraser covered is still obvious.

Bennington

DIRECTIONS: Bennington battlefield is 40 miles east of Albany on NY-67 (off US-4), a mile beyond Walloomsac (where a brass plaque commemorates Breymann's defeat).

DETAILS: The site covers Baum's Redoubt only – the other defenses have been built over – but

Baum's limited line of sight and the proximity of the tree-line to the north are clear. A bronze relief-map illustrates the routes of Stark's units. Eight miles south-east (VT-67, then VT-67A and VT-7) lies Old Bennington. The 'battle monument' marks the site of the storehouse Baum intended to capture; the museum contains relics of the battle, and the cemetery by the Old First Church has dead from both sides.

Lake George

Lake George township, at the south end of the lake, near I-87 (J21 or 22), includes the reconstructed Fort William Henry and the site of Fort George, and visitors can reach Ticonderoga by car (US-9N north) or pleasure boat.

Burgoyne's Road

Although 'Burgoyne's Road' has disappeared, it is possible to cover much of the route. Whitehall (formerly Skenesboro) on US-4 (and US-22 south from Ticonderoga) contains several museums, an arsenal, and a marina (once Skene's Mills, birthplace of Arnold's Valcour Island fleet). From Whitehall, head south on US-4 through Fort Ann (the blockhouse is a modern bank) to Hudson Falls, where the cemetery contains the grave of Jane McCrea. This road parallels the old portage road around Glens Falls. Next is Fort Edward. A park marks the site of the fort – the gift shop was built in 1776 from the fort's timbers (which was why Schuyler abandoned it). Seven miles on is Fort Miller, tastefully described as the 'site of the Jane McCrea massacre'.

Fort Stanwix / Schuyler

ADDRESS:
Fort Stanwix National Monument
112 East Park Street
Rome, New York 13440

DIRECTIONS: Fort Stanwix National Monument is located in downtown Rome, New York, 35 miles east of Syracuse and 20 miles west of Utica. Rome can be reached by car, bus, train or plane. If traveling by car, all major state routes pass through Rome: 26, 46, 49, 69, and 365, pass within sight of the Monument. To get to Rome from the New York Thruway, take exit 32 at Westmoreland to Rt. 233 north to Rt. 365 west, following the signs to downtown Rome. City parking is available within sight of the Monument. A bus terminal is within two blocks of the site on Liberty Street.

There is an AMTRAK railroad station located within one mile of the site at Lawrence Street and Route 233. If traveling by air, the nearest airport is Oneida County Airport, 8 miles south of Rome.

DETAILS: Fort Stanwix National Monument maintains an extensive archaeological collection and is the most complete reconstruction from scratch of a colonial fort in North America, with only the ravelin and some minor works missing.

Visitors begin their tour of Fort Stanwix National Monument on the path to the fort, walking the Great Oneida Carrying Place. Once inside the Visitor Center, visitors receive an orientation from the ranger on duty. After hearing and seeing some of the background history and drama of the events that happened at Fort Stanwix, you can join a ranger-led interpretive program. Other activities in the fort include living history programs. Visitors can watch a military drill demonstration and experience the blast and smoke of 18th-century weaponry. The largest exhibit at Fort Stanwix National Monument is the fort itself. By exploring this Living History Exhibit visitors can experience the sights, sounds, smells and touch of the 18th century and glimpse into the lives and events of the people who lived here more than two centuries ago. The Monument has 3 short trails that encircle the fort. One of the trails follows a portion of the Oneida Carrying Place. The other two trails interpret the events of the siege of 1777.

PROGRAMS AND ACTIVITIES: Park rangers conduct regularly scheduled interpretive programs daily, averaging 45 minutes long. Check with the ranger on duty in the Visitor Center for times and locations of all programs. Typical examples include 18th century cultural living history programs conducted daily in period clothing, military drill and musket drill and musket firing demonstrations daily, and artillery drill and firing demonstrations weekends June through August.

OPENING AND ADMISSIONS: Open daily 9.00 to 17.00, April 1 through December 31; closed Thanksgiving Day and December 25, and January 1 through March 31. There is an admission charge, but children 16 years or younger enter free. Most activities are outdoors. Good, walking shoes with closed toes and low heels are advised. Holders of Golden Eagle, Golden Age, and Golden Access Passports, and educational groups (with approved fee waiver), also enter for free.

OTHER FACILITIES: Hotels and motels are within walking distance of the site. Camping facilities are within a 15 minute drive of the site. Restaurants, convenience stores, and fuel are all within sight of the Monument. Note: picnicking facilities are not available at the fort. Due to the authenticity of the site's reconstruction, accessibility for those with special needs is limited. The Visitor Center, Museum, and rest rooms are accessible. Natural lighting is used in the living history areas of the site, resulting in dimly lit rooms.

Oriskany

Some 10 miles south-east of Rome, between NY-365 and NY-291, lies the Oriskany battlefield. Heavily farmed for two centuries, the lack of trees reveals the terrain but has lost the claustrophobic landscape of the forest. A section of military road is re-created in one corner, and a small clearing nearby contains memorials to Herkimer's colonels. Route NY-5, along the north bank of the Mohawk River from Rome to Albany, passes many historic sites and buildings from the Revolutionary and French and Indian Wars.

Saratoga National Historical Park

ADDRESS:

Saratoga National Historical Park
648 Route 32
Stillwater, NY 12170-1604

DIRECTIONS: Saratoga National Historical Park is located 40 miles north of Albany, the state capital, and some 15 miles south-east of Saratoga Springs. The principal exit (#12) off the Northway (I-87) is clearly signed for the park. The nearest airport with regularly scheduled flights is Albany. Train service is provided by AMTRAK to Saratoga Springs. To reach the park by motor vehicle:

From Montreal and points north – leave the Northway (I-87) at Exit 14 and follow signs for Route 29 East to Schuylerville where the Schuyler House and Saratoga Monument are located. Eight miles south on Route 4 you will find the main entrance to the Battlefield.

From Albany and points south – leave the Northway (I-87) at Exit 12, and follow the park signs to the Battlefield.

From points east or west – use Route 29 to Schuylerville.

Transportation within the battlefield is by personal vehicle, by foot, or by bicycle.

DETAILS: First authorized as a New York state park in 1927 on the sesquicentennial of the battles, the

Battlefield was made part of the National Park System in 1938 when Saratoga National Historical Park was authorized by the United States Congress. The park comprises three separate units, the four-square-mile battlefield in Stillwater, New York, the General Philip Schuyler House eight miles north in Schuylerville and the Saratoga Monument in the nearby village of Victory.

The park visitor center at the battlefield has an information desk and bookstore staffed year round. A 20-minute introductory film is shown every half-hour to orient visitors. A small museum contains artefacts from the time of the battles including the original 'Surrender Cannons'.

The Battlefield Tour Road is a single-lane one-way road that loops through the American defensive positions, then the actual battle sites, and finishes at the British defensive positions overlooking the Hudson River. There are ten interpretive stops along the road including the Neilson House which served as the headquarters of the American generals during the battles. This, the only surviving 1777 structure on the battlefield, is staffed by costumed park guides during the summer months and is the scene of regularly scheduled military encampments and demonstrations.

There are also some six miles of historic road traces suitable for hiking. Please contact the visitor center prior to use as trail conditions may vary depending on weather and park maintenance activities. A trail map is available at the information desk.

OPENING AND ADMISSIONS: The Battlefield Visitor Center in Stillwater is open daily from 9.00 to 17.00 except for Thanksgiving, Christmas, and New Year's Day when the park is closed. The Tour Road is open usually from April 1 to mid-November depending upon weather conditions. The Schuyler House is open for guided tours Wednesday through Sunday, 10.00 to 16.30, from June through Labor Day. An annual Schedule of Special Events is available from the park. These programs are subject to change or cancellation so calling ahead for up-to-date information on specific events is recommended.

An admission fee is charged to visit the park: however, there is no charge to visit the General Philip Schuyler House or the Saratoga Monument.

OTHER FACILITIES: There are no facilities maintained by the park for camping or lodging but there are nearby private campgrounds, hotels, motels, and bed and breakfasts. During the racing season at Saratoga (end of July and all of August) few lodging vacancies will be found in this area. There are a few restaurants, grocery stores, and gas stations located in the vicinity of the park. Directions can be obtained at the Visitor Center information desk.

SPECIAL NEEDS: A special access road up to the Visitor Center starts at the beginning of the parking lot where the picnic area is located. This leads up to a small parking lot next to the Visitor Center where a suitable paved pathway connects to the main entrance.

Schuylerville (formerly Saratoga)

Schuylerville (formerly Saratoga), just past the Schuyler mansion, was rebuilt in November 1777. Across the bridge and to the right is a memorial to an 'unknown soldier and his horse'. To the left, half-way up Burgoyne Road, is the site of the main British camp and the Battle Monument. Turning right onto NY-29, just before the main bridge over the Hudson, is Fort Hardy Park, scene of Burgoyne's 'surrender', and at the north end of the village (US-4) is 'Stark's Knob'.

The Hudson Highlands

Clinton's route from New York City can be followed on US-9W, which hugs the west bank of the Hudson River. From Tappan See Bridge (I-87/287), drive past the narrows between Verplanck's Point and Stony Point (do tour the site of Wayne's famous attack in 1779), then up Bear Mountain for an impressive view over the river and the sites of the forts. On to West Point, whose defenses were built in 1778 to prevent further British excursions up-river and which displays British guns taken at Saratoga. Ten miles north is Newburgh, where the Continental Army was disbanded in 1783: 40 miles on from here lies Kingston (formerly Esopus). From Kingston, Albany is 50 miles on US-9W or I-87, an hour's drive – the difference between victory and defeat!

INDEX

(References to illustrations are shown in **bold**. Suffix "n" = footnote.)